Pocket Rough Guide

# LISBON

written and researched by

## MATTHEW HANCOCK

# Contents

<< SUNSET OVER ALFAMA
< TRAM #28

# INTRODUCTION TO

# LISBON

Set across a series of hills overlooking the broad estuary of the Rio Tejo (River Tagus), Lisbon's stunning location and effortless beauty immediately strike most first-time visitors. It's an instantly likeable place, a big city, with a population of around two million, but one that remains human enough in pace and scale to be easily taken in over a long weekend. That said, many visitors visit again and again, smitten by a combination of old-world charm and cosmopolitan vibrancy that makes it one of Europe's most exciting cities.

RUA AUGUSTA, BAIXA

## Best place for alfresco dining

The best way to soak up Lisbon's atmosphere is to grab an outdoor table and sit back with a coffee or something more substantial. Hidden in the heart of the Alfama, *Lautasco* has tables in a tranquil courtyard (see p.48), or enjoy a pizza-with-a-view at riverside *Casanova* (see p.48). It is harder to find a lovelier lunch spot than the gardens of the Museu Nacional de Arte Antiga (see p.78), though if you want a bit of street life, *Andorra* is the place to people-watch (see p.35). Alternatively, head to one of Lisbon's squares or *miradouros* (viewpoints), many of which provide kiosk cafés.

Although now one of the EU's least expensive capitals, Lisbon was once one of the continent's wealthiest, controlling a maritime empire that stretched from Brazil to Macau. The iconic Torre de Belém, Mosteiro dos Jerónimos and dramatic Moorish castle survive from these times, though many other buildings were destroyed in the Great Earthquake of 1755. Today, much of the historic centre – the Baixa, Chiado and Bairro Alto – dates from the late eighteenth and nineteenth centuries. The biggest attraction in these quarters is the street life: nothing beats watching the city's comings and goings from a pavement café over a powerful bica coffee or Portuguese beer.

If you're fit enough to negotiate its hills, Lisbon is a great place to explore on foot: get off the beaten track and you'll find atmospheric neighbourhoods sheltering aromatic *pastelarias* (patisseries), traditional shops, and shuttered houses faced with beautiful azulejo tiles. Getting around by public transport can be fun in itself, whether you're cranking uphill on one of the city's ancient trams, riding a ferry across the Rio Tejo, or speeding across town on the metro, whose stations are decorated with adventurous contemporary art.

Lisbon also boasts excellent museums – from the Gulbenkian, with its amazing collection of arts through the ages, to the Berardo, whose modern paintings are the envy of Europe, via the Museu Nacional de Arte Antiga, the national gallery, with top

## When to visit

Lisbon is comfortably warm from April to October (average daily temperature 20–28ºC), with cooling Atlantic breezes making it less hot than Mediterranean cities on the same latitude. Most Lisbon residents take their holidays in July and August (27–28ºC), which means that some shops, bars and restaurants close for the period and the local beaches are heaving. Lower temperatures of 22–26ºC mean September and October are good times to visit, as is June, when the city enjoys its main festivals. Even in midwinter it is rarely cold and, as one of Europe's sunniest capitals, the sun usually appears at some stage to light up the city.

Portuguese and European masterpieces.

Lisbon's eclectic nightlife scene ranges from the traditional fado clubs of the Alfama district to glitzy venues in the Bairro Alto or Santos, many of them playing African and Brazilian beats influenced by immigrants from Portugal's former colonies.

Elsewhere, the city offers a fascinating mishmash of the traditional and cutting edge: chequered tiled bars full of old-timers supping brandies adjacent to boutiquey clubs pumping out the latest sounds; tiny *tascas* with bargain menus scrawled on boards rubbing shoulders with designer restaurants eyeing the latest Michelin awards, and tiny stores that wrap handmade products in paper and string overlooking gleaming shopping malls.

Should city life begin to pall, take the train out to the beautiful hill-top town of Sintra whose lush wooded heights and royal palaces comprise a UNESCO World Heritage Site. Alternatively, the lively resorts of Estoril and Cascais are just half an hour away, with the best beaches lying south of the city, along the Costa da Caparica, where Atlantic breakers crash on kilometre after kilometre of superb dune-backed sands.

SANTA ENGRÁCIA

# LISBON AT A GLANCE

## >> EATING

You are never far from a restaurant in Lisbon. For diversity, head to the **Bairro Alto** district where you'll find an eclectic array of inexpensive diners alongside ultra-hip venues. The **Baixa** caters to Lisbon's workers and has a whole street, Rua das Portas de Santo Antão, largely given over to seafood restaurants. International flavours can be sampled by the Tejo at the **Parque das Nações** and the dockside developments at **Santa Apolónia** and **Doca de Santo Amaro**, while fashionistas head to the cool haunts of **Santos**. Some of the best dining experiences, however, are in local neighbourhood restaurants highlighted in the guide.

## >> DRINKING

The most historic cafés are scattered throughout the **Baixa** and **Chiado** districts where you'll find locals getting their caffeine fixes throughout the day. You can also get beer, wine or food at these places, though many bars only open after dark (see below). Portuguese beers – largely Sagres and Superbock – are inexpensive and recommended, while local wines are invariably excellent. Worth sampling too are local brandies; the white variety of port, which makes an excellent aperitif; and a powerful cherry brandy called *ginginha* – several bars in the Baixa specialize in the stuff. Finally, don't miss trying a *caipirinha*, a Brazilian cocktail made from distilled sugar cane, sugar and lime juice.

## >> SHOPPING

Suburban Lisbon has some of Europe's largest shopping malls, but the city centre is a pleasing mixture of quirky local stores and smaller independent outlets. The top end of **Avenida da Liberdade** features the likes of Armani and Luis Vuitton, while **Chiado** is the place to head for glass and jewellery. Antique shops cluster round **São Bento**, **Príncipe Real** and **Campo de Santa Clara**, while off-the-wall clothing and accessories are to be found in the independent boutiques of the **Bairro Alto**. **Santos** has become the district of design, with several stores dedicated to contemporary jewellery and cutting-edge home products.

## >> NIGHTLIFE

Lisbon has a pulsating nightlife, with the highest concentration of clubs and bars in the **Bairro Alto**. Many locals prefer the less frenetic vibe of the **Santos** district which has a handful of cool clubs and happening bars, while the city's biggest clubs are to be found near the river, especially Lux near **Santa Apolónia** and the upmarket venues of **Alcântara**. There are various excellent live music venues, with the **Bairro Alto** and **Alfama** famed for their fado houses.

**OUR RECOMMENDATIONS FOR WHERE TO EAT, DRINK AND SHOP ARE LISTED AT THE END OF EACH PLACES CHAPTER.**

# **Day One** in Lisbon

**Café Suiça** > p.37. Join the bustle of the central square's best café, the best place to people-watch.

**2 The Baixa** > p.30. Head down main Rua da Augusta and explore the characterful streets and cafés of the Baixa grid.

**3 Chiado** > p.52. Stroll up Rua do Carmo and Rua Garrett where many of Lisbon's best shops can be found.

**Lunch** > p.57. at *Casa Liège*, where local workers fill up on hearty cuisine.

**4 Tram #28** > p.45. This is Lisbon's most famous tram route, grinding back through the Baixa and up towards the Castelo through the Alfama.

**5 Castelo de São Jorge** > p.42. Walk up to the ruined Moorish castle, the heart of historic Lisbon.

**6 Alfama** > p.45. Take the steps into the Alfama, Lisbon's village within a city where traditional life still holds sway.

**7 Casa do Fado** > p.46. Gain an insight into the history and sounds of Portugal's distinctive music at this informative museum.

**Dinner** > p.51. Try one of the Alfama's fado houses, where you can dine while listening to live music; *A Baiuca* is a good place to start.

**Drinks** > p.50. End the night by the riverside at *Lux*, one of Europe's coolest clubs.

# **Day Two** in Lisbon

**1 Museu Calouste Gulbenkian** > p.99. Take the metro to this superb museum displaying arts and crafts from the time of the Ancient Egyptians to the French Impressionists.

**2 Parque Eduardo VII** > p.100. It is a short walk from the museums to Lisbon's main central park famed for its Estufas – hothouses filled with exotic plants.

**3 Cais do Sodré** > p.54. Take the metro or a bus to Cais do Sodré where you'll find the Mercado da Ribeira, Lisbon's main market.

 **Lunch** > p.57. Have an inexpensive lunch at the ever-popular *Comida da Ribeira*, with produce fresh from the market below.

**4 Mosteiro dos Jerónimos** > p.87. Take the tram to Belém's fantastic monastery, built to give thanks to the success of Portugal's great navigators.

**5 Berardo Collection** > p.89. Don't miss this superb collection of modern art, featuring the likes of Andy Warhol and Paula Rego.

**6 Torre de Belém** > p.90. Climb the elaborate sixteenth-century riverside tower that has become the symbol of the city.

**Dinner** > p.67. *Cervejaria Trindade*, a cavernous beer hall serving great seafood.

**Drinks** > p.70. Stick around the Bairro Alto and wait for the nightlife to crank up at its hundreds of little bars and clubs.

# Lisbon **viewpoints**

Built on seven hills, Lisbon has some fantastic miradouros, or viewpoints, each with its own distinctive outlook over the city's skyline – here we list the best, along with some other dramatic vantage points.

**1 Miradouro da Santa Luzia**
> p.42. The best place to see over the terracotta rooftops of the Alfama and the eastern riverfront.

**2 São Vicente de Fora** > p.44. Climb to the top of this historic church for dizzy views over the eastern city from its extensive roof.

**3 Castelo** > p.42. Not quite Lisbon's highest hill, but climb around the ramparts to see all sides of the city.

**4 Parque Eduardo VII** > p.100. The top of the park offers an exhilarating panorama encompassing Lisbon and beyond.

**🍴 Lunch** > p.104. Chill out by a lake at *A Linha d'Água*, which serves good-value buffet lunches at the top of the park.

**5 Miradouro da Graça** > p.44. Superb views over the Castelo and the city beyond can be had from this breezy terrace by the church of Graça.

**6 Miradouro de São Pedro de Alcântara** > p.60. A broad, tree-lined

viewpoint from where you can gaze down on the Baixa and the castle opposite.

**7 Miradouro de Santa Catarina**. > p.54. Tucked-away *miradouro* with sweeping views over the Tejo, a popular hangout for Lisbon's alternative crowd.

**🍴 Dinner** > p.58. *Noobai* is hidden under the lip of Miradouro de Santa Catarina and serves inexpensive food and drinks.

# Lisbon **for families**

Lisbon is very family-friendly and children are welcomed everywhere. Below are some of the best attractions for those with kids of any age.

**1 Tram rides** > p.45. Take the famous tram #28 for the classic run, though the other routes can be just as fun with fewer crowds.

**2 Oceanário** > p.108. One of the largest in Europe, this stunning building has sharks, rays, otters, penguins and fish galore.

**3 Pavilhão do Conhecimento** > p.108. This science museum has fantastic hands-on experiments and challenges for people of all ages, together with informative exhibits.

**Lunch** > p.111. The traffic-free restaurants of Parque das Nações are great for kids – one of the best places for an inexpensive lunch is *Azul Profundo*.

**4 Boat trips** > p.142. Take a leisurely cruise up the Tejo to see the city from the river.

**5 Museu da Marioneta** > p.77. From medieval marionettes to contemporary satirical puppets, this museum trumpets an art form that satisfied children long before computer games.

**6 Caparica** > p.125. Lisbon's best beaches are just south of the city, great at any time of the year for a walk or day by the sea.

**7 Sintra** > p.112. Horse and carriage rides, castles and fantasy palaces make this a great day out for any family.

**8 Jardim Zoológico** > p.101. Along with the usual array of caged beasties, you'll find rides, games and even a cable car to peer down from.

**Dinner** > p.35. With lots of space, early-opening *Bom Jardim* has tables inside and out, affordable food that kids love, and waiters who are usually extremely child-friendly.

BEST OF LISBON

# The big sights

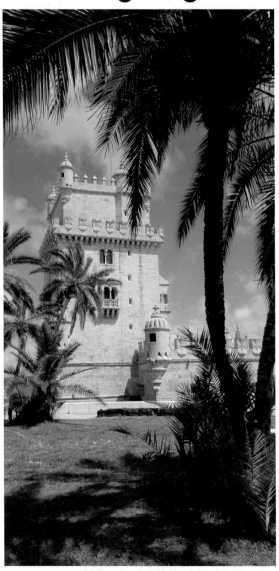

**1 Torre de Belém** This fabulously ornate tower was built to defend the mouth of the Tejo River and is now the tourist board's icon for Lisbon. > **p.90**

**2 Mosteiro dos Jerónimos** Packed with flamboyant Manueline architectural features, this sixteenth-century monastery commemorates Vasco da Gama's discovery of a sea route to India. > **p.87**

**3 Castelo de São Jorge** Once a Moorish castle and later a palace and prison, the *castelo* is now one of Lisbon's best viewpoints. > **p.42**

**4 Alfama** A maze of steps and tortuous alleys where life continues much as it has for centuries. > **p.45**

**5 Oceanário** A spectacular oceanarium, with a massive high-tech central tank containing everything from sea otters to sharks. > **p.108**

# Museums and galleries

**1** **Museu Calouste Gulbenkian** Virtually an A–Z of the history of art, from the Mesopotamians to the Impressionists, all set in a delightful park. > **p.99**

**2** **Berardo Collection** See work by some of the biggest names in modern art from Bacon to Rothko, amassed by wealthy Madeiran Joe Berardo. **> p.89**

**3** **Museu da Marinha** A giant overview of the Portuguese maritime explorations, battles and boats from replicas to full-size galleons. **> p.88**

**4** **Museu Nacional de Arte Antiga** Portugal's national gallery includes works by the likes of Nuno Gonçalves and Hieronymus Bosch. **> p.76**

**5** **Casa das Histórias** Cascais' museum building is every bit as stunning as its works of art by vibrant Portuguese contemporary artist Paula Rego. **> p.124**

# Eating out

**1 Cervejaria da Trindade** The nineteenth-century beer hall is touristy but appealing, with decorative tiles, a little garden and tasty seafood. **> p.67**

**2 Ribadouro**
Bustling restaurant specializing in superb grilled prawns, though other dishes are equally tasty. **> p.104**

**3 Tavares** Lisbon's oldest and grandest restaurant also boasts a Michelin Star. **> p.58**

**4 Bom Jardim, Rei dos Frangos**
Not exactly glamorous but the best place in town for delicious barbecue-grilled chicken. **> p.35**

**5 Rêsto do Chapitô** Buzzing tapas bar/restaurant with one of the best views in the city from its outdoor terrace. **> p.50**

# Nightlife

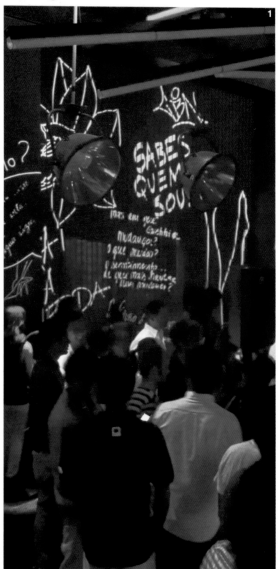

**1 Lux** Part-owned by John Malkovich and attracting international DJs, this is Lisbon's top club – it also boasts a beautiful rooftop terrace. ➤ **p.50**

**2 Casas de Fado** There are countless fado houses, mostly in the Bairro Alto or Alfama; *Adega do Ribatejo* is a great place to start. > **p.73**

**3 Enoteca** This hidden wine bar has cool stone rooms in a cavernous former bathhouse. > **p.70**

**4 A Ginginha** Tiny bar serving *ginginha* (cherry brandy) since 1840: order it with or without the stone to kick start an evening out. > **p.37**

**5 Portas Largas** Ancient *tasca* (tavern) with original marble counter and tables, but a distinctly modern clientele often spilling out onto the street. > **p.72**

# Cafés

**1** **Antiga Confeitaria de Belém** This cavernous place serves the best *pastéis de nata* in town – get there early to beat the queues. **> p.93**

**2 Suiça**
Perennially popular café with outdoor tables facing Lisbon's two main squares.
**> p.37**

**3 Café Versailles** Wonderful café with waiters in bow ties and a fleet of coiffured women devouring cakes and sandwiches. **> p.105**

**4 A Brasileira** The city's most famous café, opened in 1905 and the hub of café society ever since. **> p.58**

**5 Pois Café** Homely, high-ceilinged café in the heart of Alfama, serving fresh food, cakes and healthy snacks and with comfy sofas to lounge on.
**> p.49**

# Shopping

**1** **Mercado da Ribeira** Pungent and colourful food market, with regional crafts, food and a restaurant upstairs. > **p.54**

**2 Armazéns do Chiado** Central Lisbon's most appealing shopping centre, with top-floor cafés offering fine city views. > **p.56**

**3 Manuel Tavares** This traditional Baixa shop is a great place to buy port, wine, local cheese and confectionery. > **p.34**

**4 Espaço Fátima Lopes** Check out the latest designer clothing at this store belonging to Lisbon's queen of fashion. > **p.66**

**5 Solar Albuquerque** You could spend hours browsing the ceramics, tiles and antiques at a shop specializing in reclaimed items from old houses. > **p.66**

# The Baixa and Rossio

The tall, imposing buildings that make up the Baixa (Lower Town, pronounced bye-sha) house some of Lisbon's most interesting shops and cafés. Many of the streets are pedestrianized and, by day, they thrum with business folk and street entertainers. When the offices close, however, the whole area is strangely quiet. Facing the river, these streets felt the full force of the 1755 earthquake that destroyed much of what was then one of Europe's wealthiest capitals. The king's minister, the Marquês de Pombal, swiftly redesigned the sector with the grid pattern that is evident today, framed by a triangle of broad squares. Praça do Comércio sits to the south, with Praça da Figueira and Rossio to the north, the latter having been the city's main square since medieval times.

## PRAÇA DO COMÉRCIO

MAP P.29, POCKET MAP E13

The beautiful, arcaded Praça do Comércio represents the climax of Pombal's design. Its classical buildings were once a royal palace and the square is centred on an exuberant bronze equestrian statue of Dom José,

ARCADE ON PRAÇA DO COMÉRCIO

monarch during the earthquake and the period of the capital's rebuilding. Two of Portugal's last royals came to a sticky end in this square: in 1908 King Carlos I and his eldest son were shot dead here, clearing the way for the declaration of the Republic two years later.

Praça do Comércio's **riverfront** provides a natural focus for the area. In the hour or two before sunset people often linger in the golden light to watch the orange ferries ply between the Estação Fluvial and Barreiro on the opposite side of the Tejo. The square is one of the main venues for the city's New Year's Eve firework festivities. It is also a major transport interchange – the starting point for tram and bus tours of the city (see p.142), as well as home to the Lisbon Welcome Centre, the city's main tourist office (see p.145). It is also the place in Lisbon you are most likely to be offered a dodgy watch or "hasheesh".

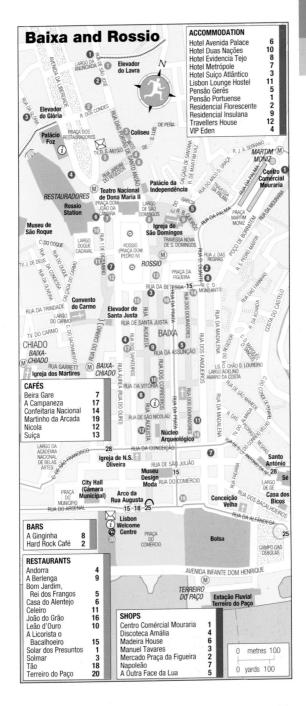

# Baixa and Rossio

## ACCOMMODATION

| | |
|---|---|
| Hotel Avenida Palace | 6 |
| Hotel Duas Nações | 10 |
| Hotel Evidencia Tejo | 8 |
| Hotel Metrópole | 7 |
| Hotel Suíço Atlântico | 3 |
| Lisbon Lounge Hostel | 11 |
| Pensão Gerês | 5 |
| Pensão Portuense | 1 |
| Residencial Florescente | 2 |
| Residencial Insulana | 9 |
| Travellers House | 12 |
| VIP Eden | 4 |

## CAFÉS

| | |
|---|---|
| Beira Gare | 7 |
| A Campaneza | 17 |
| Confeitaria Nacional | 14 |
| Martinho da Arcada | 19 |
| Nicola | 12 |
| Suíça | 13 |

## BARS

| | |
|---|---|
| A Ginginha | 8 |
| Hard Rock Café | 2 |

## RESTAURANTS

| | |
|---|---|
| Andorra | 4 |
| A Berlenga | 9 |
| Bom Jardim, Rei dos Frangos | 5 |
| Casa do Alentejo | 6 |
| Celeiro | 11 |
| João do Grão | 16 |
| Leão d'Ouro | 10 |
| A Licorista o Bacalhoeiro | 15 |
| Solar dos Presuntos | 1 |
| Solmar | 3 |
| Tão | 18 |
| Terreiro do Paço | 20 |

## SHOPS

| | |
|---|---|
| Centro Comercial Mouraria | 1 |
| Discoteca Amália | 4 |
| Madeira House | 3 |
| Manuel Tavares | 6 |
| Mercado Praça da Figueira | 2 |
| Napoleão | 7 |
| A Outra Face da Lua | 5 |

## PRAÇA DO MUNICÍPIO

MAP P.29, POCKET MAP D13

The attractive, mosaic-paved Praça do Município houses the Neoclassical nineteenth-century Câmara Municipal (City Hall), where the Portuguese Republic was declared in 1910, flatteringly described by Portugal's greatest twentieth-century poet Pessoa as "one of the finest buildings in the city". The square adjoins Rua do Arsenal, an atmospheric street packed with pungent shops selling dried cod and grocers selling cheap wines, port and brandies.

## ARCO DA RUA AUGUSTA AND RUA AUGUSTA

MAP P.29, POCKET MAP D11

Praça do Comércio's most prominent building is a huge arch, the Arco da Rua Augusta, adorned with statues of historical figures, including the Marquês de Pombal and Vasco da Gama. Acting as a gateway to the city, the arch was built to celebrate Lisbon's recon-struction after the earthquake, although it wasn't completed until 1873. From here, the mosaic-paved Rua Augusta is the Baixa's main pedestrianized thoroughfare, filled with shops, cafés, market stalls and buskers.

## MUSEU DESIGN MODA

Rua Augusta 24 ☎ 218 886 117, 🕐 www .mude.pt. Tues–Thurs & Sun 10am–8pm, Fri–Sat 10am–10pm. Free. MAP P.29, POCKET MAP E13

Housed in a grand former bank, the Museu Design Moda is an impressive collection of design and fashion classics from the 1930s to today amassed by former stockbroker and media mogul Francisco Capelo. The museum includes many of the exhibits from the former Museu do Design in Belém, such as furniture

by Charles and Ray Eames and Phillipe Starck, and has expanded to include Capelo's fashion collection – haute couture from the 1950s, 1960s street fashion and the brand labelling of the 1990s. Look out for Ron Arad's "Big Easy" steel chair (1951), Frank Gehry's wiggle chair (1972) and the 1959 Vespa, while fashionistas will adore Paco Rabanne's metalized leather boots, Pierre Cardin's 1950s coats and Alexander McQueen's superb fur skirt. There's also a bookshop and café.

## THE BAIXA GRID

MAP P.29, POCKET MAP D11

Pombal designed the Baixa to have three main streets dissected by nine smaller streets. Many of these streets took their names from the crafts and businesses carried out there, like Rua da Prata (Silversmiths' Street) and Rua dos Sapateiros (Cobblers' Street). Modern banks and offices have disturbed these divisions somewhat, though plenty of traditional stores remain; the central section of Rua da Conceição, for example, is still lined with shops selling

## The Lisbon Earthquake

Early eighteenth-century Lisbon had been one of the most active and important ports in Europe, making the Great Earthquake of 1755 all the more tragic. The quake, which was felt as far away as Jamaica, struck Lisbon at 9.30am on November 1 (All Saints' Day), when most of the city's population was at Mass. Within the space of ten minutes there had been three major tremors and the candles of a hundred church altars had started fires that raged throughout the capital. A vast tidal wave later swept the waterfront and, in all, 40,000 of the 270,000 population died. The destruction of the city shocked the continent and prompted religious debate between philosophers Voltaire and Rousseau. For Portugal, it was a disaster that ended its capital's golden age.

beads and sequins. Some of the most interesting streets to explore are the smaller ones running south to north – Rua dos Correeiros, Rua dos Douradores and Rua dos Sapateiros. Pombal also wanted the grid's churches to blend in with his harmonious design, so much so that they are almost invisible – walk along Rua de São Julião and the facade of the church of Oliveira is barely distinguishable from the offices alongside it, though its tiled interior is delightful.

### NÚCLEO ARQUEOLÓGICO

Rua dos Correeiros 9 ☎ 211 131 004. Advance bookings required. Thurs 5pm, Sat 10am–noon & 3–5pm. Free. MAP P.29, POCKET MAP E12

One of Lisbon's smallest but most fascinating museums lies beneath the Baixa's streets. The remains of Roman fish-preserving tanks, a fifth-century Christian burial place and Moorish ceramics can all be seen in the tiny Núcleo Arqueológico, containing the remains of excavations revealed during building work on the BCP bank. Most exhibits are viewed through glass floors or from cramped walkways under the modern bank during a 30- to 45-minute tour. Pombal actually rebuilt most of the Baixa on a riverbed, and you can even see the wooden piles driven into the waterlogged soil to support the buildings, the same device that is used in Venice.

## ELEVADOR DE SANTA JUSTA

Rua de Santa Justa. Daily: Oct–May 7am–10pm, June–Sept 7am–11pm. €1.40 single. MAP P.29, POCKET MAP D11

Raul Mésnier's extraordinary and eccentric Elevador de Santa Justa was built in 1902 by a disciple of Eiffel. Its giant lift whisks you 32m up the inside of a latticework metal tower, to deposit you on a platform high above the Baixa. Before taking the upper exit on to the Largo do Carmo (see p.61), head up the dizzy spiral staircase to the pricey rooftop café with great views over the city.

## ROSSIO

MAP P.29, POCKET MAP C11

Praça Dom Pedro IV (popularly known as Rossio) has been the city's main square since medieval times and it remains the hub of commercial Lisbon. Its central space sparkles with Baroque fountains and polished, mosaic-cobbled pavements. During the nineteenth century, Rossio's plethora of cafés attracted Lisbon's painters and writers, though many of the artists' haunts were converted to banks in the 1970s. Nevertheless, the outdoor seats of the square's remaining cafés are perennially popular meeting points. On the northwestern side of the square, there's a horseshoe-shaped entrance to Rossio station, a mock-Manueline complex with the train platforms an escalator ride above the street-level entrances.

## TEATRO NACIONAL DE DONA MARIA II

Rossio ☎ 213 472 246, ⓦ www.teatro-dmaria .pt. MAP P.29, POCKET MAP D10

Rossio's biggest concession to grandeur is the Teatro Nacional de Dona Maria II built along its north side in the 1840s, and heavily restored after a fire in 1964. Inside there is a good café. Prior to the earthquake, the Inquisitional Palace stood on this site, in front of which public hangings and autos-da-fé (ritual burnings of heretics) took place.

## IGREJA DE SÃO DOMINGOS

Largo de São Domingos. MAP P.29, POCKET MAP D11

The Igreja de São Domingos stands on the site of the thirteenth-century Convento de São Domingos, where sentences were read out during the Inquisition. The convent was destroyed in the earthquake of 1755, though its portal was reconstructed soon after as part of the current Dominican church. For over a century it was the venue for royal marriages and christenings, though it lost this role after the declaration of the Republic and was then gutted by a fire in the 1950s. Some say the fire purged some unsavoury acts that took place on the spot in the past, such as the massacre of New Christians which began here in 1506. It was reopened in 1997 after partial restoration to replace the seats and some statues; however, the rest of the cavernous interior and the scarred pillars remain powerfully atmospheric.

## PRAÇA DA FIGUEIRA

MAP P.29, POCKET MAP D11

Praça da Figueira is an historic square (once the site of Lisbon's main market), though the recent addition of an underground car park has detracted from its former grandeur. Nevertheless, it is slightly quieter than Rossio, and its cafés offer appealing views of the green slopes of the Castelo de São Jorge.

## PRAÇA DOS RESTAURADORES

MAP P.29, POCKET MAP C10

The elongated Praça dos Restauradores (Square of the Restorers) takes its name from the renewal of independence from Spain in 1640. To the north of the square, the **Elevador da Glória** offers access to the Bairro Alto (see p.60); south sits the superb Art Deco frontage of the old Eden cinema, now an apartment-hotel (see p.131). The square is dominated by the pink Palácio de Foz on the western side, which housed the Ministry of Propaganda under the Salazar regime (1932–74) but is now home to the Portuguese Tourist Office (see p.145) and tourist police station. During the week it is sometimes possible to visit the palace's ornate upper floors (enquire at the tourist office).

## RUA DAS PORTAS DE SANTO ANTÃO

MAP P.29, POCKET MAP D10

The pedestrianized Rua das Portas de Santo Antão is

well known for its seafood restaurants. Despite the tourist trappings – this and the adjacent Rua Jardim Regedor are the only places in town you're likely to get waiters trying to smooth-talk you into their premises – it is worth eating here at least once to sample its seafood. The street is also home to several theatres, and the domed **Coliseu dos Recreios** at #96 (☎213 240 580, ⓦwww.coliseulisboa.com), which opened in 1890 as a circus but is now one of Lisbon's main concert venues.

## ELEVADOR DO LAVRA

Largo da Anunciada. Mon-Sat 7am-9pm, Sun 9am-9pm. €1.40. MAP P.29, POCKET MAP K5

Rua das Portas de Santo Antão ends next to where another of the city's classic *elevadores*, Elevador do Lavra, begins its ascent. The funicular opened in 1882 and is Lisbon's least tourist-frequented *elevador*. At the top a short walk down Travessa do Torel takes you to **Jardim do Torel**, a tiny park offering exhilarating views over the city.

ELEVADOR DO LAVRA

# Shops

### CENTRO COMÉRCIAL MOURARIA

Largo Martim Moniz. Most shops Mon–Sat 10am–7pm. MAP P.29, POCKET MAP E10

The rather drab concrete expanse of Largo Martim Moniz – named after a Christian knight who died battling the Moors – is enlivened by the city's tackiest and most run-down shopping centre, sufficiently atmospheric to warrant a look around its six levels (three of them underground). Hundreds of small, family-run stores selling Indian fabrics and oriental and African produce, alongside an aromatic collection of cafés on Level –3, give an insight into Lisbon's ethnic communities, perfect if you need an Afro haircut or a sari.

### DISCOTECA AMÁLIA

Rua Aurea 272. Mon–Sat 9.30am–1pm & 2.30–7pm. MAP P.29, POCKET MAP D12

A small but well-stocked shop named after famous fado singer Amália Rodrigues, with a good collection of traditional Portuguese fado music. If you're looking for a recommendation, the English-speaking staff are usually happy to help.

### MADEIRA HOUSE

Rua Augusta 133. Mon–Fri 9am–1pm & 3–7pm, Sat 9am–1pm. MAP P.29, POCKET MAP D12

As you'd expect, linens and embroidery from Madeira feature, along with some attractive ceramics, tiles and souvenirs from the mainland.

### MANUEL TAVARES

Rua da Betesga 1a. Mon–Sat 9.30am–7.30pm. MAP P.29, POCKET MAP D11

Small, century-old treasure-trove, with a great selection of nuts, chocolate and national cheeses, and a basement stuffed with vintage wines and ports, some dating from the early 1900s.

### MERCADO PRAÇA DA FIGUEIRA

Praça da Figueira 10b. Mon–Fri 8.30am–8pm, Sat 8.30am–7pm. MAP P.29, POCKET MAP E11

The decorative, narrow entrance hall gives onto a well-stocked supermarket with a good array of inexpensive wines, ports and fresh produce.

### NAPOLEÃO

Rua dos Fanqueiros 70. Mon–Sat 9.30am–8pm. MAP P.29, POCKET MAP E12

This spruce shop offers a great range of quality port and wine from all Portugal's main regions, and its enthusiastic, English-speaking staff can advise on what to buy.

### A OUTRA FACE DA LUA

Rua da Assunção 22. Mon–Sat 10am–8pm. MAP P.29, POCKET MAP D12

This buzzy space specializes in retro fashion – fab clothes, tin toys and the like; it also has a great attached café serving *crostini* and snacks.

MERCADO PRAÇA DA FIGUEIRA

# Restaurants

## ANDORRA

Rua das Portas de Santo Antão 82. ☎ 213 426 047. Daily noon–midnight. MAP P.29, POCKET MAP D10

Boasting an outdoor terrace on one of the broadest stretches of the street, this is the perfect place for people-watching and remains perennially popular with tourists. The Portuguese fish dishes and grills are good but slightly overpriced, with mains ranging from €8 to €12.

## A BERLENGA

Rua Barros Queiroz 29. ☎ 213 422 703. Daily noon–11.30pm. MAP P.29, POCKET MAP D10

Atmospheric *cervejaria* with a window displaying crabs and seafood. Take a seat for a plate of prawns at the bar on one side, or sit down at the main restaurant for good-value fish, meat and seafood. Mains range from €8 to €12.

## BOM JARDIM, REI DOS FRANGOS

Trav. de Santo Antão 11–18 ☎ 213 424 389. Daily noon–11.30pm. MAP P.29, POCKET MAP C10

A bit of a Lisbon institution thanks to its spit-roast chickens and now so popular that it has spread into three buildings on either side of a pedestrianized alley. There are plenty of tables outdoors, too. A half chicken is yours for around €6, though it also serves other meat and fish at less generous prices.

## CASA DO ALENTEJO

Rua das Portas de Santo Antão 58 ☎ 213 469 231. Daily noon–3pm & 7–11pm. MAP P.29, POCKET MAP D10

A centre dedicated to Alentejan culture with its own restaurant, "Alentejo House" has an extravagantly decorated interior complete with a stunning inner courtyard and seventeenth-century furniture.

CASA DO ALENTEJO

Alentejo specialities include *sopa à alentejana* (garlic soup with egg) and *carne de porco à alentejana* (grilled pork with clams) with mains from €10; or just pop in for a drink in the superb bar area hung with chandeliers.

## CELEIRO

Rua 1° de Dezembro 65 ☎ 213 422 463. Mon–Sat noon–6pm, café 8am–6pm. MAP P.29, POCKET MAP D11

Just off Rossio, this inexpensive self-service restaurant sits in the basement of a health-food supermarket and offers tasty vegetarian spring rolls, quiches, pizza and the like from around €6. There's also a streetside café offering snacks and drinks.

## JOÃO DO GRÃO

Rua dos Correeiros 220–228 ☎ 213 424 757. Daily noon–3.30pm & 6–11pm. MAP P.29, POCKET MAP D11

One of the best in a row of restaurants on this pedestrianized street, where appealing outdoor tables tempt you to sample the reasonably priced salads, fish and rice dishes (from €8). The marble- and azulejo-clad interior is just as attractive.

### LEÃO D'OURO

Rua 1° de Dezembro 105 ☎ 213 426 195.
Daily noon–2pm & 7pm–midnight. MAP P.29,
POCKET MAP C11

Attractive azulejo-covered
restaurant, specializing in
quality seafood – the central
display groans under the
weight of the stuff. Dinner
reservations are advised,
especially for Wednesday
evening fado. Mains from €13.

### A LICORISTA O BACALHOEIRO

Rua dos Sapateiros 222–224 ☎ 213 431 415.
Mon–Fri 8am–8pm, Sat 8am–1pm. MAP P.29,
POCKET MAP D11

This pleasant tile-and-brick
restaurant is a popular lunchtime stop, when locals flock in
for inexpensive set meals or
mains from around €8.

### SOLAR DOS PRESUNTOS

Rua das Portas de Santo Antão 150 ☎ 213
424 253. Mon–Fri 12.30–3.30pm & 7–11pm.
MAP P.29, POCKET MAP J5

The "Manor House of Hams"
is, not surprisingly, best known
for its smoked ham from the
Minho region in northern
Portugal, served cold as a
starter. There are also excellent, if expensive, rice and
game dishes, not to mention
a good wine list; the service
can be overly formal. The daily
specials are good value, otherwise mains start at around €16.
Reservations are advised.

### SOLMAR

Rua das Portas de Santo Antão 108 ☎ 213
423 371. Daily noon–3pm & 7–10pm. MAP
P.29, POCKET MAP D10

A cavernous seafood restaurant,
complete with fountain and
marine mosaics, worth a visit as
much for the experience as for
the food, which can be hit or
miss. Splash out on one of the
lobsters in the bubbling tanks
and you shouldn't leave disap-

pointed. Despite the high prices
(most mains over €10), it's not
above showing live football on
giant TV screens.

### TÃO

Rua dos Douradores 10 ☎ 218 850 046.
Mon–Fri noon–3.30pm & 6.30–10pm. MAP P.29,
POCKET MAP E12

Fashionable, very good value
eastern-inspired vegetarian
restaurant, with set meals from
around €6. Tasty vegetarian
sushi, risottos, grilled auber-
gines and salads.

### TERREIRO DO PAÇO

Praça do Comércio ☎ 210 312 850. Mon–Fri
noon–3pm & 8–11pm, Sat 8–11pm, Sun
noon–5pm. MAP P.29, POCKET MAP D13

Expensive but stylish restaurant
right on the square serving
high-quality dishes such as
caramelized duck with ginger
and Azorean tuna with mango
compote, accompanied by
wine served in glasses the
size of pumpkins. Downstairs
tables are separated by wooden
screens, though the nicest
tables are in the cavernous,
brick-vaulted upstairs room.
Mains from €25. Reservations
are advised.

# Cafés

### BEIRA GARE

Rua 1° de Dezembro 5. Mon–Sat
6.30am–1am. MAP P.29, POCKET MAP D11

Well-established café opposite
Rossio station, serving stand-up
Portuguese snacks and bargain
meals. Constantly busy, which
is recommendation enough.

### A CAMPANEZA

Rua dos Sapateiros 157. Mon–Sat 8am–7pm.
MAP P.29, POCKET MAP D12

Formerly a *leitaria* (dairy shop)
and still displaying the decor
from its past existence, this is

MARTINHO DA ARCADA

### NICOLA

Rossio 24. Mon–Sat 9am–10pm, Sun 10am–7pm. MAP P.29, POCKET MAP D11

The only surviving Rossio coffee house from the seventeenth century, once the haunt of some of Lisbon's great literary figures. The outdoor tables overlooking the bustle of Rossio are the best feature, though it has sacrificed much of its period interior in the name of modernization. Also has a basement restaurant.

### SUÍÇA

Rossio 96. Daily 7am–9pm. MAP P.29, POCKET MAP D11

Famous for its cakes and pastries; you'll have a hard job getting an outdoor table here, though there's plenty of room inside. There's more alfresco seating in Praça da Figueira.

now a simple *pastelaria* (pastry shop), with decent inexpensive snacks and coffee.

### CONFEITARIA NACIONAL

Praça da Figueira 18. Daily 8am–8pm, Oct–April closed Sun. MAP P.29, POCKET MAP D11

Opened in 1829 and little changed since, with a stand-up counter selling pastries and sweets below a mirrored ceiling. There's a little side room and outdoor seating for sit-down coffees and snacks.

### MARTINHO DA ARCADA

Praça do Comércio 3. Mon–Sat 7am–11pm. MAP P.29, POCKET MAP E13

One of Lisbon's oldest café-restaurants, first opened in 1782 and declared a national monument as long ago as 1910. Over the years it has been a gambling den, a meeting place for political dissidents and, later, a more reputable hangout for politicians, writers and artists. It is now divided into a simple stand-up café and a slightly pricey restaurant. The outdoor tables under the arches are a perfect spot for a coffee and a *pastel de nata*.

# Bars

### A GINGINHA

Largo de São Domingos 8. Daily 9am–10.30pm. MAP P.29, POCKET MAP D11

Everyone should try *ginginha* – Portuguese cherry brandy – once. There's just about room in this microscopic joint to walk in, down a glassful and stagger outside to see the city in a new light.

### HARD ROCK CAFÉ

Avenida da Liberdade 2. Sun–Thurs 11am–2am, Fri & Sat 11am–4am. MAP P.29, POCKET MAP C10

Peppered with rock memorabilia and complete with an upside-down car on the roof, the interior is quite a sight. It extends to the full height of the old Condes cinema from which it was hollowed out. Enjoy a drink here, though the food, pricey burgers and steaks, is standard chain fare.

# The Sé, Castelo and Alfama

East of the Baixa, the streets climb past the city's ancient cathedral, or Sé, to the dramatic remains of the Castelo de São Jorge, an oasis of tranquillity high above the city. East of the castle lie two of Lisbon's most prominent churches, São Vicente de Fora and Santa Engrácia. The districts around the castle – Mouraria, Santa Cruz and particularly the Alfama – represent the oldest and most atmospheric parts of Lisbon. Down on the riverfront, Santa Apolónia, the main international train station, is situated in a revitalized area that boasts the glitzy Lux club and some fine restaurants, a short bus ride from a fascinating tile museum.

## THE SÉ

Largo da Sé ☎ 218 866 752. Daily 10am–7pm. Free. Tram#28. MAP P.40-41, POCKET MAP F12

Lisbon's main cathedral, the Sé, was founded in 1150 to commemorate the city's Reconquest from the Moors on the site of their main mosque. It's a Romanesque structure with a

THE SÉ CATHEDRAL

suitably fortress-like appearance. The great rose window and twin towers form a simple and effective facade, although there's nothing particularly exciting inside: the building was once splendidly embellished on the orders of Dom João V, but his Rococo whims were swept away by the 1755 earthquake and subsequent restorers. All that remains is a group of Gothic tombs behind the high altar and the decaying thirteenth-century **cloister** (Mon–Sat 10am–7pm, Sun 2–7pm; €2.50). This is currently being heavily excavated, revealing the remains of a sixth-century Roman house and Moorish public buildings. The Baroque **Treasury** (Mon–Sat 10am–5pm; €2.50) holds a small museum of treasures including the relics of Saint Vincent, brought to Lisbon in 1173 in a boat that was piloted by ravens, according to legend. Ravens were kept in the cloisters for centuries afterwards, but the tradition halted when the last one died in 1978. To this day, the birds remain one of the city's symbols.

## IGREJA DE SANTO ANTÓNIO AND MUSEU ANTONIANO

Largo S. António da Sé ☎ 218 860 447. Tram #28. MAP P.40-41, POCKET MAP E12

The eighteenth-century church of **Santo António** (open daily) is said to have been built on the spot where the city's most popular saint was born as Fernando Bulhões; after his death in Italy he became known as Saint Anthony of Padua. The tiny neighbouring **museum** (Tues–Sat 10am–1pm & 2–6pm, Sun 10am–1pm; €1.50, free Sun) chronicles the saint's life, including his enviable skill at fixing marriages, though only devotees will find interest in the statues and endless images.

## CASA DOS BICOS

Rua dos Bacalhoeiros ☎ 218 810 900. Open for exhibitions only. Entry varies. MAP P.40-41, POCKET MAP F13

The Casa dos Bicos means the "House of Points", and its curious walls – set with diamond-shaped stones – give an idea of the richness of pre-1755 Lisbon. It was built in 1523 for the son of the Viceroy of India, though only the facade of the original building survived the earthquake. It is in fairly regular use as the venue for cultural exhibitions when you can also see the remains of Roman fish-preserving tanks and parts of Lisbon's old Moorish walls (demolished in the fifteenth century).

## Tram #25 to Prazeres

The open area to the south of the Casa dos Bicos is the terminus for another of Lisbon's classic tram rides, the #25 (Mon–Fri every 15 mins from 7am–9pm), which sees far fewer tourists than tram #28 (see p.45) but takes almost as picturesque a route. From here it trundles along the riverfront and up through Lapa and Estrela to the suburb of Prazeres, best known as the site of one of Lisbon's largest cemeteries. You can stroll round the enormous plot where family tombs are movingly adorned with trinkets and photos of the deceased.

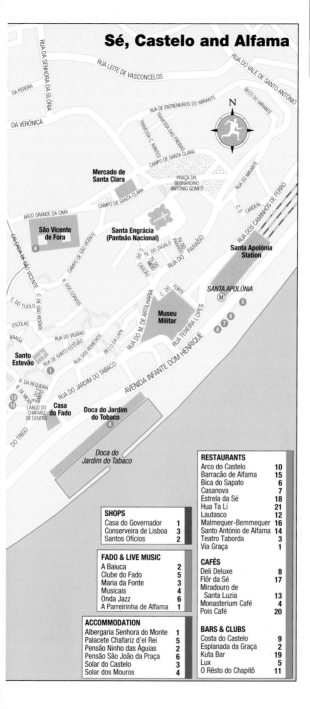

# Sé, Castelo and Alfama

**SHOPS**

| | |
|---|---|
| Casa do Governador | 1 |
| Conserveira de Lisboa | 3 |
| Santos Ofícios | 2 |

**FADO & LIVE MUSIC**

| | |
|---|---|
| A Baiuca | 2 |
| Clube do Fado | 5 |
| Maria da Fonte | 3 |
| Musicais | 4 |
| Onda Jazz | 6 |
| A Parreirinha de Alfama | 1 |

**ACCOMMODATION**

| | |
|---|---|
| Albergaria Senhora do Monte | 1 |
| Palacete Chafariz d'el Rei | 5 |
| Pensão Ninho das Águias | 2 |
| Pensão São João da Praça | 6 |
| Solar do Castelo | 3 |
| Solar dos Mouros | 4 |

**RESTAURANTS**

| | |
|---|---|
| Arco do Castelo | 10 |
| Barracão de Alfama | 15 |
| Bica do Sapato | 6 |
| Casanova | 7 |
| Estrela da Sé | 18 |
| Hua Ta Li | 21 |
| Lautasco | 12 |
| Malmequer-Bemmequer | 16 |
| Santo António de Alfama | 14 |
| Teatro Taborda | 3 |
| Vía Graça | 1 |

**CAFÉS**

| | |
|---|---|
| Deli Deluxe | 8 |
| Flôr da Sé | 17 |
| Miradouro de Santa Luzia | 13 |
| Monasterium Café | 4 |
| Pois Café | 20 |

**BARS & CLUBS**

| | |
|---|---|
| Costa do Castelo | 9 |
| Esplanada da Graça | 2 |
| Kuta Bar | 19 |
| Lux | 5 |
| O Rêsto do Chapitô | 11 |

## MUSEU DO TEATRO ROMANO

Entrance on Patio de Aljube 5 ☎ 218 820 320, Ⓦ www.museu-teatroromano.net. Tues–Sun 10am–1pm & 2–6pm. Free. Tram #28. MAP P.40-41, POCKET MAP F12

The Museu do Teatro Romano displays a wealth of Roman coins, spoons and fragments of pots, statues and columns excavated from the ruins of a Roman theatre, dating from 57 AD, which are fenced off just north of Rua Augusto Rosa. Roman Lisbon – Olisipo – became the administrative capital of Lusitania, the western part of Iberia, under Julius Caesar in 60 BC, and the theatre shows the wealth that quickly grew thanks to its fish-preserving industries.

## MIRADOURO DE SANTA LUZIA

MAP P.40-41, POCKET MAP F12

The church of Santa Luzia marks the entry to the Miradouro de Santa Luzia, a spectacular viewpoint where elderly Lisboetas play cards and tourists gather to take in the sweeping views across the Alfama and the river beyond.

MUSEU DE ARTES DECORATIVAS

## MUSEU DE ARTES DECORATIVAS

Museum Largo das Portas do Sol 2 ☎ 218 814 600, Ⓦ www.fress.pt. Mon & Wed–Sun 10am–5pm. €4. Tram #28. MAP P.40-41, POCKET MAP F11

Set in the seventeenth-century Azurara Palace, this fascinating museum contains some of the best examples of sixteenth- to eighteenth-century applied art in the country. Founded by a wealthy banker and donated to the nation in 1953, the museum boasts unique pieces of furniture, major collections of gold, silver and porcelain, magnificent paintings and textiles. The rambling building covers five floors, set around a stairway decorated with spectacular azulejos. Highlights include a stunning sixteenth-century tapestry depicting a parade of giraffes, beautiful carpets from Arraiolos in the Alentejo district, and oriental-influenced quilts that were all the rage during the seventeenth and eighteenth centuries. The museum also has a small café with a patio garden.

## CASTELO DE SÃO JORGE

☎ 218 800 620, Ⓦ www.castelosaojorge-egeac.pt. Daily: March–Oct 9am–9pm; Nov–Feb 9am–6pm. €5 includes visit to Câmara Escura and Olisipónia. Bus #37 from Praça da Figueira. MAP P.40-41, POCKET MAP F11

Reached by a confusing but well-signposted series of twisting roads, the Castelo de São Jorge is perhaps the most spectacular building in Lisbon, as much because of its position as anything else. Now Lisbon's most-visited tourist site, the castle's was once the heart of a walled city that spread downhill as far as the river. The original Moorish castle on this site was besieged in 1147 by a particularly ruthless gang of Crusaders who, together with King Alfonso I of Portugal, conquered Lisbon after some four hundred years of Moorish rule. Badly damaged during the siege, its fortifications were rebuilt. From the fourteenth century, Portuguese kings took up residence in the old Moorish palace, or Alcáçova, within the walls, but by the early sixteenth century they had moved to the new royal palace on Praça do Comércio. Subsequently, the castle was used as a prison and then as an army barracks until the 1920s. The walls were partly renovated by Salazar in the 1930s and further restored for the Expo 98. A series of gardens, walkways and **viewpoints** hidden within the old Moorish walls makes this an enjoyable place in which to wander about for a couple of hours, with spectacular views over the city from its ramparts and towers.

CASTELO DE SÃO JORGE VIEWPOINT

## CÂMARA ESCURA

Castelo de São Jorge. Weather permitting daily: March–Oct, 10am–8.30pm; Nov–Feb 10am–5pm. MAP P.40–41, POCKET MAP F11

One of the castle towers, the Tower of Ulysses, now holds a kind of periscope which projects sights from around the city onto a white disk with commentary in English. Unless you like being holed up in dark chambers with up to fifteen other people, though, you may prefer to see the view in the open air.

## THE ALCÁÇOVA AND OLISIPÓNIA

Castelo de São Jorge. Daily: March–Oct 10am–5pm; Nov–Feb 9am–5.30pm. MAP P.40–41, POCKET MAP F11

Only a much-restored shell remains of the old Moorish Alcáçova. This now houses Olisipónia, a multimedia history of Lisbon shown in three underground chambers. Portable headsets provide a .

35-minute commentary on aspects of Lisbon's development; although the presentations overlap somewhat and gloss over a few of Lisbon's less savoury chapters, such as slavery and the Inquisition, they are a useful introduction to the city.

## SANTA CRUZ AND MOURARIA

Castelo de São Jorge. MAP P.40–41, POCKET MAP F11

Crammed within the castle's outer walls is the tiny medieval quarter of Santa Cruz. This remains a village in its own right, with its own school, bathhouse and church. Leaving Santa Cruz, a tiny arch at the end of Rua do Chão da Feira leads through to Rua dos Cegos and down to Largo Rodrigues de Freitas, which marks the eastern edge of Mouraria, the district to which the Moors were relegated after the siege of Lisbon – hence the name. Today Mouraria is an atmospheric residential area with some of the city's best African restaurants, especially around Largo de São Cristóvão.

SANTA ENGRÁCIA

## MIRADOURO DA GRAÇA

MAP P.40-41, POCKET MAP F10

The Miradouro da Graça provides superb views over Lisbon and the castle. To reach it take Tram #28 (see p.45) to the broad Largo da Graça. From here, head past Nossa Senhora da Graça – a church which partly dates from 1271, making it one of the oldest in the city – to the viewpoint which also has a small kiosk café-bar (see p.50).

## SÃO VICENTE DE FORA

Tues–Sun 10am–6pm. Church free, monastery €4. Tram #28. MAP P.40-41, POCKET MAP G11

The church of São Vicente de Fora stands as a reminder of the extent of the sixteenth-century city; its name means "Saint Vincent of the Outside". It was built during the years of Spanish rule by Philip II's Italian architect, Felipe Terzi (1582–1629); its geometric facade was an important Renaissance innovation. Of more interest is the adjoining monastery. Through the beautiful cloisters, decorated with azulejos representing scenes from Portugal's history, you can visit the old monastic refectory, which since 1855 has

formed the pantheon of the Bragança dynasty. Here, in more or less complete sequence, are the **tombs** of all the Portuguese kings from João IV, who restored the monarchy in 1640, to Manuel II, the last Portuguese monarch who died in exile in England in 1932. Among them is Catherine of Bragança, the widow of England's Charles II, who is credited with introducing the concept of "teatime" to the British. If you have energy, climb to the roof for spectacular views out over the city. There's also a lovely café by the entrance if you do fancy a cup of tea.

## FEIRA DA LADRA

Tues and Sat 9am–around 3pm. Tram #28.
MAP P.40-41, POCKET MAP H10

The broad, leafy square of Campo de Santa Clara is home to the twice-weekly Feira da Ladra ("Thieves' Market"), Lisbon's main flea market. It's not the world's greatest market, but it does turn up some interesting things, like oddities from the former African colonies and old Portuguese prints. Out-and-out junk – from broken alarm clocks to old postcards – is spread on the ground above Santa Engrácia, with cheap clothes, CDs and half-genuine antiques at the top end of the *feira*. The covered *mercado* (market) building has a fine array of fresh fruit and vegetables.

## SANTA ENGRÁCIA

Campo de Santa Clara. Tues–Sun: May–Oct 10am–6pm; Nov–April 10am–5pm. €3. Tram #28. MAP P.40-41, POCKET MAP H10

The white dome of Santa Engrácia makes it the loftiest church in the city, and it has become synonymous with unfinished work – begun in 1682, it was only completed in 1966. It is now the **Panteão Nacional**, housing the tombs of eminent Portuguese figures, including writer Almeida Garrett (1799–1854) and Amália Rodrigues (1920–99), Portugal's most famous fado singer. You can take the stairs up to the terrace, from where there are great views over eastern Lisbon.

## THE ALFAMA

MAP P.40-41, POCKET MAP G12

In Moorish times, the Alfama was the grandest part of the city, but as Lisbon expanded, the new Christian nobility moved out, leaving it to the local fishing community. None of today's houses dates from before the Christian

IGREJA DE SÃO MIGUEL, ALFAMA

Reconquest, but you'll notice a kasbah-like layout. Although an increasing number of fado restaurants are moving in, the quarter retains a quiet, village-like quality. Life continues much as it has done for years in the labyrinthine streets, with people buying groceries and fish from hole-in-the-wall stores and householders stoking small outdoor charcoal grills. Half the fun of exploring here is getting lost, but at some point head for Rua de São Miguel – off which run some of the most interesting *becos* (alleys) – and for the parallel street Rua de São Pedro, where *varinas* (fishwives) sell the catch of the day from tiny stalls.

## Tram #28

The picture-book tram #28 is one of the city's greatest rides, though its popularity is such that there are usually queues to get on and standing room only is more than likely. Built in England in the early twentieth century, the trams are all polished wood and chrome but give a distinctly rough ride up and down Lisbon's steepest streets, at times coming so close to shops that you could almost take a can of sardines off the shelves. From Graça, the tram plunges down through Alfama to the Baixa and up to Prazeres, to the west of the centre. Take care of belongings as pickpockets also enjoy the ride.

## CASA DO FADO E DA GUITARRA PORTUGUESA

Largo do Chafariz de Dentro ☎ 218 823 470, ⓦ www.museudofado-egeac.pt. Tues–Sun 10am–6pm. €3. MAP P.40-41, POCKET MAP G12

Set in the renovated Recinto da Praia, a former water cistern and bathhouse, the Casa do Fado e da Guitarra Portuguesa provides an excellent introduction to this quintessentially Portuguese art form (for more on fado see the box, p.51). The museum details the history of fado and its importance to the Portuguese people; its shop stocks a great selection of CDs. A series of rooms in the museum contains wax models, photographs, famous paintings of fado scenes and descriptions of the leading singers. It also traces the history of the Portuguese guitar, an essential element of the fado performance. Interactive displays allow you to listen to the different types of fado (Lisbon has its own kind, differing from that of the northern city of Coimbra), varying from mournful to positively racy.

TILE DETAIL, MUSEU NACIONAL DO AZULEJO

## DOCA DO JARDIM DO TOBACO

Bus #28, 35 or 794 from Praça do Comércio. MAP P.40-41, POCKET MAP H12

On the riverfront lies the dockland development of the Doca do Jardim do Tobaco. Its name, "Tobacco Garden Dock", refers to its previous role as the city's main depot for storing tobacco. Facing one of the broadest sections of the Rio Tejo, it's a great place for a sunset drink or an evening meal, its restaurants and bars attracting a largely local if well-to-do crowd.

## MUSEU NACIONAL DO AZULEJO

Rua da Madre de Deus 4 ☎ 218 103 340, ⓦ www.mnazulejo-ipmuseus.pt. Tues 2–6pm, Wed–Sun 10am–6pm. €4, free Sun 10am–2pm. Bus #794 from Praça do Comércio/Santa Apolónia. MAP P.40-41, POCKET MAP M5

The Museu Nacional do Azulejo (tile museum) traces the development of Portuguese azulejo tiles from fifteenth-century Moorish styles to the present day, with each room representing a different period. Diverse styles range from seventeenth-century portraits of the English King Charles II with his Portuguese wife, Catherine of Bragança, to the 1720 satirical panel depicting a man being given an injection in his bottom. The museum is inside the church Madre de Deus, whose eighteenth-century tiled scenes of St Anthony are among the best in the city. Many of the rooms are housed round the church's cloisters – look for the spire in one corner of the main cloister, itself completely tiled. The highlight upstairs is Portugal's longest azulejo – a wonderfully detailed 40-metre panorama of Lisbon, completed in around 1738. The museum also has a good café-restaurant and shop.

CONSERVEIRA DE LISBOA

somewhat touristy collection of regional crafts, but including some attractive ceramics, rugs, embroidery, baskets and toys.

# Restaurants

### ARCO DO CASTELO

Rua do Chão da Feira 25 ☎ 218 876 598. Mon–Sat noon–midnight. MAP P.40-41, POCKET MAP F12

Cheerful place just below the entrance to the castle, specializing in moderately priced Goan dishes – choose from tempting shrimp curry, Indian sausage or spicy seafood. Mains are from €9.

### BARRACÃO DE ALFAMA

Rua de S. Pedro 16 ☎ 218 866 359. Daily 11am–midnight. MAP P.40-41, POCKET MAP G12

An unpretentious tiled local tasca popular with locals, with non-touristy prices: you can have a full meal here for under €15. Portions are generous with fine fish and grills from under €7. There are a few outdoor tables at the back in summer.

### BICA DO SAPATO

Avda Infante Dom Henrique, Armazém B, Cais da Pedra à Bica do Sapato ☎ 218 810 320. Mon 7pm–midnight, Tues–Sat 12.30pm–midnight. MAP P.40-41, POCKET MAP M6

This stylish yet informal warehouse conversion has mirrored walls to reflect the crisp Tejo vistas. There's an outside terrace, too. The chef creates what he calls a "laboratory of Portuguese ingredients", including hare with rice and a fabulous "crustacean mix" of crabs and tiger prawns as well as pasta and sushi. Satisfied guests have included Pedro Almodóvar, Catherine Deneuve and architect Frank Gehry, though its prices (mains around €15) are affordable to mere mortals.

# Shops

### CASA DO GOVERNADOR

Castelo de São Jorge. Daily 10am–6pm. MAP P.40-41, POCKET MAP F11

Right by the castle entrance, the former Governor of Lisbon's house is now a shop with a somewhat sparse and eclectic collection of art books, black-and-white postcards of old Lisbon, fado and world music CDs, and some tasteful ceramics.

### CONSERVEIRA DE LISBOA

Rua dos Bacalhoeiras 34. Mon–Fri 9am–noon & 1–7pm, Sat 9.30am–1pm. MAP P.40-41, POCKET MAP E13

Wall-to-wall tin cans stuffed into wooden cabinets make this colourful 1930s shop a bizarre but intriguing place to stock up on tinned sardines, squid, salmon, mussels and just about any other sea beast you can think of.

### SANTOS OFÍCIOS

Rua da Madalena 87. Mon–Sat 10am–8pm. MAP P.40-41, POCKET MAP E12

Small shop crammed with a

## CASANOVA

Avda Infante Dom Henrique, Loja 7 Armazém B, Cais da Pedra à Bica do Sapato ☎ 218 877 532. Tues 6pm–1.30am, Wed–Sun 12.30pm–1.30am. MAP P.40–41, POCKET MAP M6

If *Bica do Sapato* is beyond your budget, the more modestly priced *Casanova* next door offers pizza, pasta and *crostini* accompanied by similar views from its outside terrace. It's phenomenally popular and you can't book, so turn up early. Expect to pay around €15 for a meal and drink.

## ESTRELA DA SÉ

Largo S. António da Sé 4 ☎ 218 870 455. Mon–Fri 9am–9pm, Sat 9am–2pm. MAP P.40–41, POCKET MAP E12

Beautiful azulejo-covered restaurant near the Sé, serving inexpensive and tasty dishes like *alheira* (chicken sausage), salmon and Spanish-style tapas. Its wooden booths – perfect for discreet trysts – date from the nineteenth century.

## HUA TA LI

Rua dos Bacalhoeiros 119 ☎ 218 879 170. Daily noon–3.30pm & 6.30–11pm. MAP P.40–41, POCKET MAP E13

Great value Chinese restaurant (mains from €6), very popular for Sunday lunch, when it heaves with diners (so it's best to book). Seafood scores highly; try the squid chop suey. It's also good for vegetarians.

## LAUTASCO

Beco do Azinhal 7 ☎ 218 860 173. Mon–Sat 10am–3pm & 9–11.30pm; closed Dec. MAP P.40–41, POCKET MAP G12

Tucked just off the Largo do Chafariz de Dentro, in a picturesque Alfama courtyard; by day a shady retreat, by night a magical, fairy-lit oasis. Multilingual menus and higher than usual prices (mains from around €12) suggest a

DELI DELUXE

largely tourist clientele but it's a great spot for *borrego* (lamb), *tamboril* (monkfish) or *cataplanas* (stews). Bookings are advised.

## MALMEQUER-BEMMEQUER

Rua de São Miguel 23–25 ☎ 218 876 535. Wed–Sun 12.30–3.30pm & 7.30–10.30pm, Tues 7.30–10.30pm; closed last week in Oct. MAP P.40–41, POCKET MAP G12

Cheerily decorated and moderately priced place, overseen by a friendly owner. Grilled meat and fish dishes dominate the menu (try the *salmão no carvão* – charcoal-grilled salmon), or eat from the daily changing tourist menu – mains €7–9.

## SANTO ANTÓNIO DE ALFAMA

Beco de São Miguel 7 ☎ 218 881 328 or 218 881 329. Daily except Tues noon–2am. MAP P.40–41, POCKET MAP G12

With a lovely outdoor terrace shaded by vines, this is one of the nicest restaurant-bars in the Alfama; it's off Rua de São Miguel; book to guarantee a table. There's a very long list of expensive wines; pasta and fish dishes from €13 or a range of less pricey tapas from €7.

### TEATRO TABORDA

Costa do Costelo 75 ☎ 218 879 484. Tues–
Sun 2pm–midnight. MAP P.40-41, POCKET MAP F10
Fashionable theatre café-
restaurant with fine views from
the terrace. The menu offers
inexpensive fish and fresh
vegetarian dishes, including
vegetable lasagne, Greek salad
and falafels from €7–8.

### VIA GRAÇA

Rua Damasceno Monteiro 9b ☎ 218 870
830. Mon–Fri 12.30–3pm & 7.30–11pm, Sat
7.30–11pm. MAP P.40-41, POCKET MAP K5
Tucked away below the
Miradouro da Graça (take a left
after Largo da Graça becomes
Rua da Graça), this smart and
expensive restaurant in an
unattractive modern building is
a whole lot better on the inside,
from where you can soak up
the stunning panoramas of
Lisbon. Specialities include
roast goat with rice and game
*cataplana* from around €15–22.

# Cafés

### DELI DELUXE

Avda Infante Dom Henrique, Armazem B, Loja
8. Tues–Fri noon–10pm, Sat 10am–10pm, Sun
10am–8pm. MAP P.40-41, POCKET MAP M6
A modern deli with delectable
cheeses, cured meats and
preserves, though the riverside
café at the back is even more
appealing. Grab a seat outdoors
and enjoy the range of goodies
from croissants to speciality
teas, yoghurts, bagels, salads
and cocktails.

### FLÔR DA SÉ

Largo da Sé. Mon–Sat 7am–8pm. MAP P.40-41,
POCKET MAP E12
Conveniently near the
cathedral, this *pastelaria* has a
counter packed with pastries
and savouries. Tables are set
out beneath azulejos depicting
Santo António. It also does
decent, inexpensive lunches.

### MIRADOURO DE SANTA LUZIA

Miradouro de Santa Luzia. Daily 9am–11pm.
MAP P.40-41, POCKET MAP F12
Hilltop suntrap just below the
viewpoint of the same name.
Drinks and meals are slightly
pricey but you pay for the
views, which are fabulous.

### MONASTERIUM CAFÉ

Igreja São Vicente de Fora, Calçada de
São Vicente ☎ 218 885 652. Tues–Sun
10am–5pm. MAP P.40-41, POCKET MAP G11
The São Vicente monastery
café boasts comfortable indoor
seating and a tranquil patio, a
lovely spot for a drink or light
lunch.

### POIS CAFÉ

Rua São João da Praça 93–95. Tues–Sun
11am–8pm. MAP P.40-41, POCKET MAP F12
With its big comfy sofas and
laid-back ambience, this high,
arched ceiling café is a must.
There's a friendly, young crowd,
books to dip into by the bare
stone walls, light meals and
home-made snacks, including a
great *apfelstrudel*.

POIS CAFÉ

# Bars and clubs

## COSTA DO CASTELO

Calçada do Marquês de Tancos 1b ☎ 218 884 636. Tues–Sat 11pm–2am, Sun 3–11pm. MAP P.40-41, POCKET MAP E11

Beautifully positioned terrace-bar/restaurant with Baixa views, a long list of cocktails and mid-priced pasta and fish dishes. Occasional live music and events, usually at weekends.

## ESPLANADA DA GRAÇA

Largo da Graça ☎ 217 217 508. Daily, weather permitting, 10am–2am. MAP P.40-41, POCKET MAP F10

A tiny kiosk serving coffee, drinks and snacks by the Miradouro da Graça. It's not cheap, but the seats have stunning views over the bridge and the Baixa, particularly at sunset. After dark, it cranks up a powerful music system to change the atmosphere from laid-back to decidedly lively.

## KUTA BAR

Trav. do Chafariz d'El Rei 8 ☎ 967 957 257. Mon–Fri 6pm–2am, Sat & Sun 6pm–4am. MAP P.40-41, POCKET MAP G12

Named after the beach resort in Bali, this striking eastern-inspired bar combines oriental decor with Parisian chic; its French owner rustles up superb cocktails and snacks. Monday and Thursday buffet nights have all-you-can-eat sushi from €20.

## LUX

Armazéns A, Cais da Pedra a Santa Apolónia ⓦ www.lux@luxfragil.com. Tues–Sun midnight–6am. MAP P.40-41, POCKET MAP M6

This converted former meat warehouse has become one of Europe's most fashionable spaces, attracting A-list visitors such as Prince and Cameron Diaz. Part-owned by actor John Malkovich, it was the first place to venture into the docks opposite Santa Apolónia station. There's a rooftop terrace with amazing views, various bars, projection screens, a frenzied downstairs dancefloor, and music from pop and trance to jazz and dance. The club is also increasingly on the circuit for touring bands.

## O RÊSTO DO CHAPITÔ

Costa do Castelo 7 ☎ 218 867 334, ⓦ www.chapito.org. Restaurant daily noon–3pm & 7.30–midnight. Bar daily noon–1.30am. MAP P.40-41, POCKET MAP E12

Multipurpose venue incorporating a theatre, circus school, restaurant and tapas bar. The restaurant is in an upstairs dining room, reached via a spiral staircase, and serves a range of menus with mains such as black pork with ginger and mushroom risotto from €9. The outdoor esplanade commands terrific views over Alfama and most people come here to drink and take in the view. Check the website for live music, films and readings.

O RÊSTO DO CHAPITÔ

# Fado and live music

## A BAIUCA

Rua de São Miguel 20 ☎ 218 867 284.
Thurs–Mon 7.30–11pm. MAP P.40–41, POCKET
MAP G12

Nightly fado is performed in this great little tiled *tasca* which serves decent fresh fish and grills from €15. Reservations advised.

## CLUBE DO FADO

Rua de São João da Praça 94 ☎ 218 852
704, ⓦ www.clube-de-fado.com. Daily
8.30pm–2am. MAP P.40–41, POCKET MAP F12

Intimate and homely fado club with stone pillars, an old well as a decorative feature, and a mainly local clientele. It attracts small-time performers, up-and-coming talent and the occasional big name. Expect to pay €50 or so including food.

## MARIA DA FONTE

Rua de São Pedro 5a ☎ 218 876 896. Tues–
Sun 8pm–2am. MAP P.40–41, POCKET MAP G12

Tiny, intimate tiled *casa do fado* with good-value fish dishes. The speciality is *bife na pedra* (steak cooked on a hot stone). Live fado from 8pm on most nights, when average prices are €25–30 a head.

## MUSICAIS

Doca do Jardim do Tobaco Pavilhão A/B
ⓦ www.musicaisbar.com. Daily noon–2am.
MAP P.40–41, POCKET MAP H12

Dockside bar with fine river views and live music most nights from 11.30pm, usually from Thursday to Sunday. Sounds range from flamenco and folk to occasional rock.

## ONDA JAZZ

Arco de Jesus 7 ☎ 218 883 242, ⓦ www
.ondajazz.com Tues–Sat 8pm–2am. MAP P.40–41,
POCKET MAP F12

One of Lisbon's best jazz clubs, with regular top acts along with local musicians. Wednesday night jamming sessions, with live shows most nights from 11pm.

## A PARREIRINHA DE ALFAMA

Beco do Espírito Santo 1 ☎ 218 868 209.
Daily 8pm–2am. MAP P.40–41, POCKET MAP G12

One of the best fado venues owned by famous fado singer Argentina Santos, just off Largo do Chafariz de Dentro, often attracting leading stars and an enthusiastic local clientele. Reservations are advised when the big names appear.

## Fado

Fado (literally "fate") is often described as a kind of Portuguese blues. Popular themes are love, death, bullfighting and indeed fate itself. It is believed to derive from music that was popular with eighteenth-century immigrants from Portugal's colonies who first settled in Alfama. Famous singers like Maria Severa and Amália Rodrigues grew up in Alfama, which since the 1930s has hosted some of the city's most authentic fado houses – stroll around after 8pm and you'll hear magical sounds emanating from various venues, or better still, enjoy a meal at one of the places we list above. The big contemporary name is Mariza, who grew up in neighbouring Mouraria. Other singers to look out for (though unlikely to appear in small venues) are Mizia, Carminho, Helder Moutinho, Carlos do Carmo, Maria da Fe and Cristina Branco.

# Chiado and Cais do Sodré

The well-to-do district of Chiado (pronounced she-ar-doo) is famed for its smart shops and cafés, along with the city's main museum for contemporary arts. Down on the waterfront, Cais do Sodré (pronounced kaiysh doo soodray) is a down-at-heel suburb. Many of its waterfront warehouses have been converted into upmarket cafés and restaurants and by day, in particular, a stroll along its characterful riverfront is very enjoyable. Nearby Mercado da Ribeira, Lisbon's main market, is also big on atmosphere, as is the hillside Bica district, which is served by another of the city's classic funicular street lifts – Elevador da Bica. Cais do Sodré is also where you can catch ferries across the Tejo to the little port of Cacilhas which not only has some great seafood restaurants with views over Lisbon, but it is also the bus terminus for some of the region's best beaches and for the spectacular Cristo Rei statue of Christ.

## RUA GARRETT

MAP P.53, POCKET MAP C12

Chiado's most famous street, Rua Garrett, is where you'll find some of the oldest shops and cafés in the city, including *A Brasileira* (see p.58). Beggars usually mark the nearby entrance to the **Igreja dos Mártires** (Church of the Martyrs), named after the English Crusaders who were killed during the siege of Lisbon. Some of the area's best shops can also be found in nearby Rua do Carmo. This was the heart of the area that was greatly damaged by a fire in 1988, although the original *belle époque* atmosphere has since been superbly recreated under the direction of eminent Portuguese architect Álvaro Siza Vieira.

RUA GARRETT

# Chiado and Cais do Sodré

## ACCOMMODATION
| | |
|---|---|
| Hotel Bairro Alto | 3 |
| Hotel Borges | 2 |
| Hotel Lisboa | |
| Regency Chiado | 1 |
| Oasis Hotel | 4 |

## SHOPS
| | |
|---|---|
| Ana Salazar | 1 |
| Armazéns do Chiado | 3 |
| Fábrica Sant'Anna | 7 |
| Livraria Bertrand | 5 |
| Loja de Artesenato | 9 |
| Livraria Ulisses | 2 |
| Storytailors | 8 |
| Torres and Brinkmann | 4 |
| A Vida Portuguesa | 6 |

## RESTAURANTS
| | |
|---|---|
| Aqui há Peixe | 1 |
| Casa Liège | 8 |
| Cervejaria Farol | 17 |
| Comida da Ribeira | 15 |
| L'Entrecôte | 11 |
| Noobai | 12 |
| Porto de Abrigo | 14 |
| Tavares | 4 |
| Yasmin | 13 |

## BARS
| | |
|---|---|
| Bicaense | 10 |
| Guarda Rio | 16 |
| Hotel Bairro Alto | 9 |
| Inter Mezo | 7 |

## CAFÉS
| | |
|---|---|
| Bernard | 5 |
| A Brasileira | 6 |
| Café Vertigo | 2 |
| Leitaria Académica | 3 |

## TEATRO NACIONAL DE SÃO CARLOS

Rua Serpa Pinto 9 ☎ 213 468 408, ⊕ www.saocarlos.pt. Café daily from 10am. MAP ABOVE. POCKET MAP C13.

Lisbon's main opera house, the Teatro Nacional de São Carlos, was built shortly after the original Lisbon opera house on Praça do Comércio was destroyed in the Great Earthquake. Heavily influenced by the leading Italian opera houses, it has a sumptuous Rococo interior, but you can only see it during performances. You can enjoy the theatre's café at other times, with pleasant outside tables surrounded by olive trees.

## Fernando Pessoa

Café *A Brasileira* is marked by a bronze statue of Fernando Pessoa (1888–1935), Portugal's greatest contemporary poet and a leading figure of twentieth century modernism. Born in Lisbon, Pessoa grew up in South Africa before returning to Portugal in 1905 to work as a translator. He spent much of his time composing poems in Lisbon's cafés. Many of his works are about identity – he wrote under various alter egos or "heteronyms", each with their own personality and style. The most famous are Alberto Caeiro, Ricardo Reis and Alvaro de Campos, though his most famous work is the *Book of Disquiet* written under the heteronym Bernardo Soares. The partly autobiographical work is full of extraordinary philosophical ruminations that have established his reputation as a leading existentialist artist.

## MUSEU DO CHIADO

Rua Serpa Pinto 4 ☎ 213 432 148. Ⓦ www.
museudochiado-ipmuseus.pt. Tues–Sun
10am–6pm. €4, free Sun 10am–2pm. MAP P.53,
POCKET MAP C13

The Museu do Chiado traces
the history of art from
Romanticism to Modernism.
It is housed in a stylish
building with a pleasant
courtyard café and rooftop
terrace, constructed around
a nineteenth-century biscuit
factory. Within the gallery's
permanent collection are
works by some of Portugal's
most influential artists since
the nineteenth century, along
with foreign artists influenced
by Portugal including Rodin.
Highlights include Almada
Negreiros' 1920s panels from
the old São Carlos cinema,
showing Felix the Cat; a
beautiful sculpture, *A Viúva*
(*The Widow*), by António
Teixeira Lopes; and some
evocative early twentieth-
century Lisbon scenes by
watercolourist Carlos Botelho.
There are also frequent temporary exhibitions.

A VIÚVA, MUSEU DO CHIADO

## MIRADOURO DE SANTA CATARINA

Tram #28. MAP P.53. POCKET MAP A12

Set on the cusp of a hill high
above the river, the railed
Miradouro de Santa Catarina
has spectacular views. Here, in
the shadow of the statue of the
Adamastor – a mythical beast
from Luís de Camões's *Lusiads*
– a mixture of oddballs and
New Age types often collects
around an alluring drinks kiosk
(daily 10am–dusk, weather
permitting), which has a few
outdoor tables.

## ELEVADOR DA BICA

Entrance on Rua de São Paulo. Mon–Sat
7am–9pm, Sun 9am–9pm. €1.40 single. MAP
P.53, POCKET MAP B13

With its entrance tucked into
an arch on Rua de São Paulo,
the Elevador da Bica is one of
the city's most atmospheric
funicular railways. Built in
1892 – and originally powered
by water counterweights, but
now electrically operated – the
*elevador* leads up towards
the Bairro Alto, via a steep
residential street. Take time to
explore the steep side streets of
the Bica neighbourhood, too, a
warren of characterful houses,
little shops and fine local
restaurants.

## MERCADO DA RIBEIRA

Main entrance on Rua Dom Luís I. Ⓦ www
.espacoribeira.pt. Main market Tues–Sat
5am–2pm. MAP P.53, POCKET MAP B13

The Mercado da Ribeira is
Lisbon's most historic market.
Built originally on the site of
an old fort at the end of the
nineteenth century, the current
structure dates only from 1930.
The market downstairs has
an impressive array of fresh
fish, fruit and vegetables, with
a separate, aromatic flower
section (open until 7pm). In
the past it was traditional for

Lisboetas to enjoy a *cacau da Ribeira* (cocoa) here after a night out on the town, and the local council recently decided to renovate the market building in an attempt to restore this social function. As a result, the upper level now boasts a shop and bustling **restaurant** (see p.57). From Wednesday to Sunday, live music ranging from jazz to folk is performed either on a central stage or in the pub-like *RibeirArte Café* in the upper level, and on Sundays there is a morning collectors' market.

## CACILHAS AND ALMADA

MAP P.53, POCKET MAP J8

The short, blustery ferry ride from Lisbon's Cais do Sodré over the Tejo to Cacilhas is great fun and grants wonderful views of the city. Cacilhas is little more than a bustling bus and ferry terminal with a pretty church, surrounded by lively stalls and cafés, but is well known for its seafood restaurants. You can also visit the **Dom Fernando II e Glória frigate** (⊙ 917 841 149; Tues–Sun 10am–5pm; €3), built in India in 1843 and now a museum showing what life at sea was like in the mid-nineteenth century. A good riverside walk to head west towards the bridge along the waterfront. It's around fifteen minutes' walk to the **Elevador Panorâmico da Boca do Vento** (daily 9.30am–7pm; €2.80 return), a sleek lift that whisks you 30m up the cliff

CRISTO REI

face to the attractive old part of Almada, giving fantastic views over the river and city.

## CRISTO REI

Bus #101 from outside the Cacilhas ferry terminal; Lift open daily: June–Sept 9.30am–7pm; Oct–May 9.30am–6.15pm; €4 return; Ⓦ www.cristorei.pt. MAP P.53, POCKET MAP H9

On the heights above Almada stand the outstretched arms of Cristo Rei, built in 1959 as a pilgrimage site to grace Portugal's non-participation in World War II. A lift at the statue shuttles you a further 80m up to a dramatic viewing platform, from where, on a clear day, you can catch a glimpse of the glistening roof of the Pena palace at Sintra.

## Travel to Cacilhas and beyond

Cais do Sodré is the main departure point for ferries over the Tejo to the largely industrial suburbs to the south. Ferries to Cacilhas (every 15mins, 5.40am–2.30am; €0.80 single) dock by a large bus and tram depot; buses run from here to Costa da Caparica (see p.125).

# Shops

### ANA SALAZAR

Rua do Carmo. Mon–Sat 10am–noon & 3–7pm. MAP P.53, POCKET MAP D11

One of Lisbon's best-known names for modern and individual designer clothes for men and women, together with bags and belts.

### ARMAZÉNS DO CHIADO

Rua do Carmo 2. Daily 10am–10pm, restaurants until 11pm. MAP P.53, POCKET MAP D12

This swish shopping centre sits on six floors above metro Baixa-Chiado in a structure that has risen from the ashes of the Chiado fire, though it retains its traditional facade. Various shops include branches of Massimo Duti (women), Sportzone, Bodyshop and the classy toy shop Imaginarium. The top floor has a series of cafés and restaurants, including Brazilian chain *Chimarrão*, most offering great views.

### FÁBRICA SANT'ANNA

Rua do Alecrim 95. Mon–Fri 9.30am–7pm, Sat 10am–2pm. MAP P.53, POCKET MAP C13

If you're interested in Portuguese azulejos, check out this factory shop, founded in 1741, which sells copies of traditional designs and a great range of ceramics.

### LIVRARIA BERTRAND

Rua Garrett 73. Mon–Thurs 9am–8pm, Fri & Sat 9am–10pm, Sun 2–10pm. MAP P.53, POCKET MAP C12

Portugal's oldest bookshop, founded in 1773 and once the meeting place for Lisbon's literary set. Offering novels in English and a range of foreign magazines, it's also a good place to find English translations of Portuguese writers including Fernando Pessoa.

STORYTAILORS

### LOJA DE ARTESENATO

Mercado da Ribeira, entrance on Avenida 24 de Julho. Daily 10am–9pm. MAP P.53, POCKET MAP B14

Upstairs in the market building, this shop specializes in art and crafts from Lisbon and the Tejo valley, with modern glassware, crafts and ceramics.

### LUVARIA ULISSES

Rua do Carmo 87a. Mon–Sat 10am–7pm. MAP P.53, POCKET MAP D11

The superb, ornately carved wooden doorway leads you into a minuscule glove shop, with hand-wear to suit all tastes tucked into rows of boxes.

### STORYTAILORS

Calçada do Ferragial 8. Tues–Sat 10am–9pm. MAP P.53, POCKET MAP C13

Set in a suitably stylish bare-brick eighteenth-century former warehouse, the shop interior is as magical as its designer clothes inspired by fairy tales. Its haute couture range has been snapped up by the likes of Madonna, Janet Jackson and Lily Allen, though you'll need a rock star's salary to afford most items.

### TORRES AND BRINKMANN

Rua Nova da Trindade 1b. Tues–Sat 9.30am–7pm, Mon 2.30–7pm. MAP P.53, POCKET MAP C12

The best place in the city to buy cookery equipment; it has stylish, high-quality pots, pans and utensils, including coffee-making gear and griddles. There's another branch just up the road at Trav. da Trindade 18–22, specializing in porcelain, glass and silverware.

### A VIDA PORTUGUESA

Rua Anchieta 11. Mon–Sat 10am–8pm. MAP P.53, POCKET MAP C12

Somewhat sparse and expensive but evocative collection of retro toys, crafts and ceramics, beautifully displayed and packaged in a historic former grocery.

# Restaurants

### AQUI HÁ PEIXE

Rua da Trindade 18a ☎ 213 432 154. Tues–Sun noon–3pm & 7–11pm. MAP P.53, POCKET MAP C12

Meaning "We've got fish here", this stylish seafood restaurant has been making waves even with Lisboetas who know a thing or two about the sea's produce. Classic fish dishes are served with panache – sublime tuna steaks, prawns cooked in garlic, clams cooked with coriander, plus a few meat dishes, all from around €15, in a neat fish-themed interior.

### CASA LIÈGE

Rua da Bica Duarte Belo 72–74 ☎ 213 422 794. Mon–Sat 11am–11pm. MAP P.53, POCKET MAP B12

Small and bustling *tasca* at the top end of the Elevador da Bica, packed at lunchtimes thanks to filling and inexpensive dishes such as grilled chicken, sausages and fine *pastéis de bacalhau* from under €7. Good house wine, too.

### CERVEJARIA FAROL

Alfredo Dinis Alex 1–3, Cacilhas ☎ 212 765 248. Daily 10am–midnight. MAP P.53, POCKET MAP H9

The most high-profile seafood restaurant in Cacilhas, with fine views across the Tejo to match. If you feel extravagant, it's hard to beat the lobsters, though other fish dishes are yours from around €9. Azulejos on the wall show the old *farol* (lighthouse) that once stood here – the restaurant is located along the quayside, on the right as you leave the ferry.

### COMIDA DA RIBEIRA

Mercado da Ribeira, entrance on Avenida 24 de Julho ☎ 213 244 980. Mon–Sat noon–3pm & 8–11.30pm. MAP P.53, POCKET MAP B14

The market's buffet restaurants are so popular they lead to lunchtime scrums – come before 12.30pm to beat the rush. From around €8, you can help yourself to dishes including squid kebabs, *bacalhau* dishes, salads and *feijoada* (bean stew), with occasional live music (usually Fridays). The à la carte menu is good value, with mains from €9.

CERVEJARIA FAROL

## L'ENTRECÔTE

Rua do Alecrim 117–120 ☎ 213 473 616.
Daily 12.30–3pm & 8pm–midnight. MAP P.53,
POCKET MAP C12

This upmarket, relaxing,
wood-panelled restaurant
with soaring ceilings has won
awards for its entrecôte steak
which is just as well, as that's
all it serves. With a sauce said
to contain 35 ingredients, it is
truly delicious. There's also a
good set menu for around €17.
Dinner reservations advised.

## NOOBAI

Miradouro de Santa Catarina ☎ 213 465
014. Mon–Sat noon–midnight. MAP P.53, POCKET
MAP A12

Modern, jazzy café-restaurant
with a superb terrace just below
Miradouro de Santa Catarina.
Fabulous views complement
the inexpensive fresh juices,
salads, quiches and the like.

## PORTO DE ABRIGO

Rua dos Remolares 16–18 ☎ 213 460 873.
Mon–Sat 11am–11pm. MAP P.53, POCKET MAP C13

This long-established restaurant
with a little stained-glass
window near the main market
serves good-value dishes such
as octopus, salmon and *açorda
de camarão* (shrimps with
garlicky bread sauce) from
around €8.

## TAVARES

Rua da Misericórdia 37 ☎ 213 421 112.
Tues–Sat 12.30–2.30pm & 7.30–11pm. MAP
P.53, POCKET MAP C12

Lisbon's oldest restaurant,
dating from 1784, is a riot
of gilt and mirrors, a fitting
setting for Michelin-starred
cooking. This is the place to try
the best of modern Portuguese
cuisine from young chef José
Avillez: seafood rice, pork
and clams or *bacalhau* dishes
from €35, or a tasting menu at
around €90.

## YASMIN

Rua da Moeda 1a ☎ 213 930 074. Mon–Sat
7.30pm–2am. MAP P.53, POCKET MAP B13

Very fashionable corner restaurant near the market specializing in creative cuisine, fusing
oriental and Mediterranean
influences with local ingredients, backed by jazzy sounds.
Expensive.

# Cafés

## BERNARD

Rua Garrett 104. Mon–Sat 8am–midnight..
MAP P.53, POCKET MAP C12

Often overlooked because of
its proximity to *A Brasileira*,
this ornate café offers superb
cakes, ice cream and coffees;
it also has an outdoor terrace
on Chiado's most fashionable
street.

## A BRASILEIRA

Rua Garrett 120. Daily 8am–2am. MAP P.53,
POCKET MAP C12

Opened in 1905, and marked
by an outdoor bronze statue

TAVARES

PESSOA STATUE, A BRASILEIRA

the ruined Carmo church. Besides drinks and snacks, it also does light lunches; in summer, the grilled sardines are hard to beat.

# Bars

### BICAENSE

Rua da Bica Duarte Belo 38–42. Mon–Sat 12.30–3pm & 8pm–2am. MAP P.53, POCKET MAP B12

Small, fashionable bar on the steep street used by the Elevador da Bica, with occasional live jazz and Latin sounds and a moderately priced bar-food menu.

### GUARDA RIO

Rua da Cintura 22. Daily 9am–midnight. MAP P.53, POCKET MAP B14

Little more than a neat wooden chalet with outdoor seats facing the river near Cais do Sodré station, this bar-restaurant is a peaceful spot for a drink by day, though it can get lively after dark when the sound system gets going. Decent fish and grills from around €9.

### HOTEL BAIRRO ALTO

Praça Luis de Camões 8. Daily noon–midnight. MAP P.53, POCKET MAP C12

Swish and stylish split-level hotel bar, with a giant triangular table in the main area, a downstairs video-room and laid-back lounge area full of comfy cushions. Pricey drinks come with generous bowls of nuts.

### INTER MEZO

Rua Garrett Patio 19. Mon–Sat 11am–11pm. MAP P.53, POCKET MAP D12

With outside seats in a hidden courtyard, this stylish little modern bar does a mean range of cocktails and other drinks; its sister *Mezo Giorno* next door also serves decent pizzas.

of the poet Fernando Pessoa, this is the most famous of Lisbon's old-style coffee houses. The tables on the pedestrianized street get snapped up by tourists but the real appeal is in its traditional interior, where prices are considerably cheaper than on the outdoor esplanade, especially if you stand at the long bar. At night buskers often add a frisson as the clientele changes to a more youthful brigade, all on the beer.

### CAFÉ VERTIGO

Travessa do Carmo 4 ☎ 213 433 112. Daily except Thursdays 10am–midnight. MAP P.53, POCKET MAP C12

An arty crowd frequents this bare-brick walled café with an ornate glass ceiling. Occasional art exhibits and a good range of cakes and snacks.

### LEITARIA ACADÉMICA

Largo do Carmo 1–3. Daily 7am–midnight. MAP P.53, POCKET MAP C12

Outdoor tables on one of the city's leafiest squares, outside

# Bairro Alto and São Bento

The Bairro Alto, the upper town, sits on a hill west of the Baixa. After the 1755 earthquake, the relatively unscathed district became the favoured haunt of Lisbon's young bohemians. Home to the Institute of Art and Design and various designer boutiques, it is still the city's most fashionable district. By day, the central grid of narrow, cobbled streets feels residential. After dark, however, the area throngs with people visiting its famed fado houses, bars and restaurants, while the city's gay community coalesces around the clubs of clubs of neighbouring Princípe Real. There are impressive monuments too including the Palácio da Assembléia, Portugal's parliamentary building in nearby São Bento. This area houses good ethnic restaurants, a legacy of the city's first black community established by the descendents of African slaves.

## ELEVADOR DA GLÓRIA

Mon–Fri 7am–midnight, Sat 8.30am–2am, Sun 9am–midnight. €1.40 single. MAP P.62–63, POCKET MAP C11

Everyone should ride the Elevador da Glória at least once. From the bottom of Calçada da Glória (off Praça dos Restauradores, see p.33), the funicular climbs the knee-jarringly sheer street in a couple of minutes, leaving the lower city behind as you ascend above its rooftops. An amazing feat of engineering, the tram system was built in 1885. It was originally powered by water displacement before this was replaced by steam before electricity was introduced.

At the top, pause at the gardens, the **Miradouro de São Pedro de Alcântara**, from where there's a superb view across the city to the castle.

ELEVADOR DA GLÓRIA

## IGREJA DE SÃO ROQUE

Largo de Trindade Coelha ☏ 213 235 382.
Mon 2–6pm, Tues–Wed & Fri–Sun 10am–6pm,
Thurs 9am–9pm. Free. MAP P.62-63, POCKET
MAP C11

The sixteenth-century Igreja de São Roque looks like the plainest church in the city, with its bleak Renaissance facade. Yet inside lies an astonishing succession of lavishly decorated side chapels. The highlight is the **Capela de São João Baptista**, for its size the most expensive chapel ever constructed. It was ordered from Rome in 1742 by Dom João V to honour his patron saint and, more dubiously, to gratify Pope Benedict XIV whom he had persuaded to confer a patriarchate on Lisbon. It was erected at the Vatican for the Pope to celebrate Mass in, before being dismantled and shipped to Lisbon at the then vast cost of £250,000. If you examine the four "oil paintings" of John the Baptist's life, you'll find that they are in fact intricately worked mosaics. The more valuable parts of the altar front are kept in the adjacent **museum** (Tues–Wed & Fri–Sun 10am–6pm, Thurs 2–9pm. €2.50, free Sun 10am–2pm), which also displays sixteenth- to eighteenth-century paintings and a motley collection of church relics.

## CONVENTO DO CARMO

Entrance on Largo do Carmo ☏ 213 478 629.
Mon–Sat: June–Sept 10am–7pm; Oct–May
10am–6pm. €3. MAP P.62-63, POCKET MAP D12

Built between 1389 and 1423, and once the largest church in the city, the Convento do Carmo was partially destroyed by the 1755 earthquake but is even more striking as a result with its beautiful Gothic arches rising grandly into the sky. Today it houses the splendid

CONVENTO DO CARMO

**Museu Arqueológico do Carmo**, home to many of the treasures from monasteries that were dissolved after the 1834 revolution. The entire nave is open to the elements, with columns and statuary scattered in all corners. Inside, on either side of what was the main altar, are the main exhibits, centring on a series of tombs. Largest is the beautifully carved, stone tomb of Ferdinand I; nearby, that of Gonçalo de Sousa, chancellor to Henry the Navigator, is topped by a statue of Gonçalo himself. There is also an Egyptian sarcophagus, whose inhabitant's feet are just visible underneath the lid; and, equally alarmingly, two pre-Columbian mummies which lie in glass cases, alongside the preserved heads of a couple of Peruvian Indians.

The exit to the **Elevador de Santa Justa** (see p.32) is at the side of the Convento do Carmo – go onto the rampway leading to it for fine views over the city.

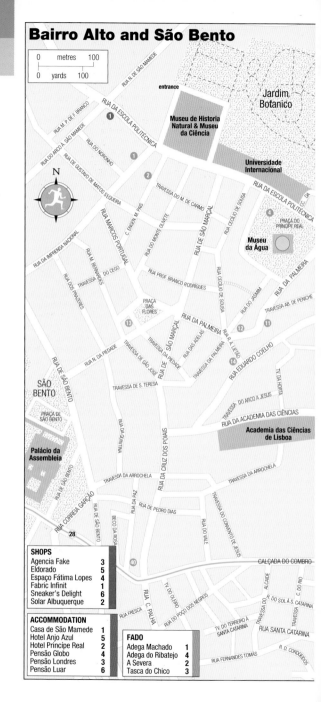

# Bairro Alto and São Bento

**SHOPS**

| | |
|---|---|
| Agencia Fake | 3 |
| Eldorado | 5 |
| Espaço Fátima Lopes | 4 |
| Fabric Infinit | 1 |
| Sneaker's Delight | 6 |
| Solar Albuquerque | 2 |

**ACCOMMODATION**

| | |
|---|---|
| Casa de São Mamede | 1 |
| Hotel Anjo Azul | 5 |
| Hotel Principe Real | 2 |
| Pensão Globo | 4 |
| Pensão Londres | 3 |
| Pensão Luar | 6 |

**FADO**

| | |
|---|---|
| Adega Machado | 1 |
| Adega do Ribatejo | 4 |
| A Severa | 2 |
| Tasca do Chico | 3 |

| CAFÉS | |
|---|---|
| Catedral do Pão | 7 |
| Pão de Canela | 13 |
| Tease | 38 |

| BARS & CLUBS | |
|---|---|
| Arroz Doce | 24 |
| Bar Ártis | 26 |
| Bedroom Bar | 22 |
| Cinco Lounge | 14 |
| Clube da Esquina | 32 |
| Enoteca | 3 |
| Finalmente | 12 |
| Frágil | 18 |
| Janela da Atalaia | 17 |
| Lisbona | 15 |
| Majong | 41 |
| Pavilhão Chinês | 8 |
| Portas Largas | 20 |
| Sétimo Céu | 33 |
| Snob | 10 |
| Solar do Vinho do Porto | 16 |
| A Tasca Tequila Bar | 19 |
| Trumps | 1 |
| Zé Dos Bois | 31 |

| RESTAURANTS | |
|---|---|
| 1º de Maio | 42 |
| Baralto | 34 |
| Bota Alta | 21 |
| Calcuta | 35 |
| O Cantinho da Bem Estar | 36 |
| Cantinho da Paz | 40 |
| Cervejaria da Trindade | 29 |
| Comida de Santo | 2 |
| Esperança | 27 |
| Esplanada | 4 |
| Faz Frio | 5 |
| Gáveas | 23 |
| Louro e Sal | 30 |
| Pap'açorda | 28 |
| La Paparrucha | 9 |
| Sinal Vermelho | 25 |
| Sul | 39 |
| Tasca do Manel | 37 |
| Tascardoso | 6 |
| Terra | 11 |

## BAIRRO ALTO

MAP P.62-63, POCKET MAP B11

Quiet by day, the graffitied central streets of the Bairro Alto buzz with people after dark, especially on summer weekends when the streets become a giant mass of partygoers. The most lively area is the tight network of streets to the west of Rua da Misericórdia, particularly after midnight in Rua do Norte, Rua Diário de Notícias, Rua da Atalaia and Rua da Rosa. Running steeply downhill, Rua do Século is one of the area's most historic streets. A sign at no. 89 marks the birthplace of the Marquês de Pombal, the minister responsible for rebuilding Lisbon after the Great Earthquake.

### PRAÇA DO PRÍNCIPE REAL

Bus #758 or 778 from Chiado. MAP P.62-63, POCKET MAP A10

North of the Bairro Alto, the streets open out around the leafy Praça do Príncipe Real, one of the city's loveliest squares. Laid out in 1860 and surrounded by the ornate homes of former aristocrats – now mostly offices – the square is the focal point of Lisbon's gay scene, though by day it is largely populated by families in the local play park or locals playing cards under the trees.

### MUSEU DA ÁGUA PRÍNCIPE REAL

Praça do Príncipe Real. Mon–Sat 10am–6pm. €2.50. Bus #758 or 778 from Chiado. MAP P.62-63, POCKET MAP A10

The Museu da Água Príncipe Real is accessed down steps in the centre of the square of the same name. Inside is an eerie nineteenth-century reservoir, where you can admire brick and vaulted ceilings, part of a network of tunnels that link up with the Aqueduto das Águas Livres (see p.98). One of the tunnels heads down through what is now the *Enoteca* wine bar (see p.70). The museum also hosts occasional temporary exhibits that you admire from a series of walkways.

### MUSEUS DE POLITÉCNICA

Rua Escola Politécnica 56. Tues–Fri 10am–5pm, Sat & Sun 11am–6pm; closed Aug; €4 for each museum or combined ticket for €10, includes entry to temporary exhibitions and Jardim Botânico. Bus #758 or 778 from Chiado. MAP P.62-63, POCKET MAP H5

The nineteenth-century Neoclassical former technical college now hosts the mildly engaging museums of science and natural history known as the Museus de Politécnica. The **Museu da Ciência** has some absorbing geological exhibits and a low-tech interactive section where you can balance balls on jets of air and swing pendulums among throngs of school kids.

The **Museu da Historia Natural** opposite, houses a rather dreary collection of stuffed animals, eggs and shells, though temporary exhibitions can be more diverting.

## JARDIM BOTÂNICO

Rua Escola Politécnica ☎ 213 921 830, 🖤 www.jb.vl.pt. May–Oct Mon–Fri 9am–8pm, Sat & Sun 10am–6pm; Nov–April Mon–Fri 9am–6pm, Sat & Sun 10am–6pm. €1.50 gardens, €2.50 includes "Lugartagis", or €10 for combined ticket to Museus de Politécnica. MAP P.62–63, POCKET MAP H5

The lush botanical gardens are almost invisible from the surrounding streets and provide a tranquil escape from the city bustle. The Portuguese explorers introduced many plant species to Europe during the golden age of exploration (from the fifteenth to eighteenth centuries) and these gardens, laid out between 1858 and 1878, are packed with twenty thousand neatly labelled species from around the world. Shady paths lead downhill under towering palms and luxuriant shrubs past a "Lugartagis" greenhouse for breeding butterflies.

## PALÁCIO DA ASSEMBLÉIA

Tram #28. MAP P.62–63, POCKET MAP H6

Below the Bairro Alto in the district of São Bento, you can't miss the late sixteenth-century Neoclassical facade of the Palácio da Assembléia. Formerly a Benedictine monastery, it was taken over by the government in 1834 and today houses the *Assembléia da República*, Portugal's **parliament**; it's not open to the public, though you can arrange a tour by special arrangement (☎ 213 919 000). Most visitors make do with the view of its steep white steps from tram #28 as it rattles along Calçada da Estrela, though it is worth exploring the surprisingly earthy streets nearby. This was where Lisbon's black community put down roots – Rua do Poço dos Negros (black man's well) takes its awful name from the corpses of slaves tossed into a hole here.

## CASA MUSEU AMÁLIA RODRIGUES

Rua de São Bento 193 ☎ 213 971 896. Tues–Sun 10am–1pm & 2–6pm. €5. Bus #706 from Praça do Comércio, or a short walk from tram #28. MAP P.62–63, POCKET MAP G6

The daughter of an Alfama orange-seller, Amália Rodrigues was the undisputed queen of fado music until her death in 1999. The house where she lived since the 1950s has been kept as it was, and you can also admire original posters advertising her performances on stage and in the cinema, portraits by Portuguese artists and some of her personal possessions.

JARDIM BOTÂNICO

# Shops

### AGENCIA FAKE

Rua do Norte 115. Shop Mon–Sat 2pm–2am.
MAP P.62–63, POCKET MAP C11

Get your hair cut, buy a new outfit and have a night out all in the same place. This designer clothes and shoe shop turns into a bar from early evening until 2am, while Agencia 117, two doors down, has more clothes and doubles as a hair salon.

### ELDORADO

Rua do Norte 115. Mon–Sat 2pm–midnight.
MAP P.62–63, POCKET MAP C12

An interesting mixture of clubbing gear and secondhand castoffs alongside old records and CDs, aimed at Lisbon's young groovers. A good place to head for if you need a new wardrobe for a night out without breaking the bank.

### ESPAÇO FÁTIMA LOPES

Rua da Atalaia 36. Mon–Fri 10am–1.30pm & 2.30–8pm, Sat 11.30am–2.30pm & 3.30–8.30pm. MAP P.62–63, POCKET MAP B12

One of the few large shops in the Bairro Alto and flagship store for the confident designs of Lisbon's top designer. Her clothes are bold and colourful, reflecting the mood of Portugal's younger generation. There's also a bar, though it's only open sporadically.

### FABRIC INFINIT

Rua Dom Pedro V 74. Tues–Sat 11am–7pm.
MAP P.62–63, POCKET MAP B10

Upmarket store selling one-off and unique designer jewellery, shoes and home products; should you tire of browsing there's an attractive café, selling organic produce, complete with Zen garden patio at the back.

SNEAKER'S DELIGHT

### SNEAKER'S DELIGHT

Rua do Norte 30–32. Mon–Sat 1–10pm. MAP P.62–63, POCKET MAP C12

A typical example of Bairro Alto creativity – limited edition sneakers and a few designer clothes in a sparse space dotted with bits of old TVs and computers that are a work of art in their own right.

### SOLAR ALBUQUERQUE

Rua Dom Pedro V 68–70. Daily 10am–7pm, closed weekends in July and Aug. MAP P.62–63, POCKET MAP B10

A huge treasure-trove of antique tiles, plates and ceramics dating back to the sixteenth century – great for a browse.

# Restaurants

### 1° DE MAIO

Rua da Atalaia 8 ☎ 213 426 840. Mon–Fri noon–3pm & 7–11pm, Sat 7–11pm. MAP P.62–63, POCKET MAP B12

Naked Chef-style food: simple slabs of grilled fish and meat with boiled veg and chips. You can watch the cook through a hatch at the back, adding to the theatrics of a bustling, traditional *adega* (wine cellar) with a low, arched ceiling. Mains are around €10. Get there early to be sure of a table.

## BARALTO

Rua do Diário de Notícias 31 ☎ 213 426 739. Mon–Sat 7pm–midnight. MAP P.62–63, POCKET MAP B12

A cosy tiled place with efficient service – along with the usual fish and meat you'll find unusual dishes such as tuna pie and duck rice from around €11.

## BOTA ALTA

Trav. da Queimada 37 ☎ 213 427 959. Mon–Fri noon–2.30pm & 7–10.30pm, Sat 7–10pm. MAP P.62–63, POCKET MAP B11

Tavern decorated with old boots (*botas*) and an eclectic picture collection. It attracts queues for its vast portions of sensibly priced traditional Portuguese food – including *bacalhau com natas* (cod cooked in cream) and fine cakes. The tables are crammed in and it's always packed; try to arrive before 8pm or book in advance. Mains from €10.

## CALCUTA

Rua do Norte 17 ☎ 213 428 295. Mon–Sat noon–3pm & 6.30–11pm. MAP P.62–63, POCKET MAP C12

Very popular Indian restaurant attracting a youngish clientele. Lots of chicken, seafood and lamb curries, tandoori dishes, and good vegetarian options with mains from around €9. Reservations are advised.

## O CANTINHO DO BEM ESTAR

Rua do Norte 46. ☎ 213 464 265. Tues–Sun 7–11pm. MAP P.62–63, POCKET MAP C12

Small and popular, the "canteen of well-being" lives up to its name: get there early to guarantee a place. From the menu, the rice dishes and generous salads are the best bet.

## CANTINHO DA PAZ

Rua da Paz 4 ☎ 213 969 698. Mon–Sat 12.30–2.30pm & 3.30–11pm. MAP P.62–63, POCKET MAP H7

Though favoured by MPs from the parliament building, this is an unpretentious Goan restaurant just off tram route #28. There's shark soup, prawn curry and a few vegetarian options on offer, served in a homely little dining room overseen by an enthusiastic owner who can guide you through the well-priced menu.

## CERVEJARIA DA TRINDADE

Rua Nova da Trindade 20 ☎ 213 423 506. Daily 9am–2am. MAP P.62–63, POCKET MAP C11

The city's oldest beer-hall dates from 1836. At busy times you'll be shown to your table; at others, avoid the dull modern extensions and find a space in the original vaulted hall, decorated with azulejos, depicting the elements and seasons. Shellfish is the speciality, though other fish and meat dishes (from €9) are lighter on the wallet. There is also a patio garden and – a rarity – a children's menu.

BOTA ALTA

## COMIDA DE SANTO

Calçada Engenheiro Miguel Pais 39 ☎ 213 963 339. Daily 12.30–3.30pm & 7.30pm–1am. MAP P.62–63, POCKET MAP H6

Late-opening, slightly pricey Brazilian restaurant serving cocktails and classic dishes such as *feijoada a brasileira* (Brazilian bean stew) and a fantastic *ensopadinho de peixe* (fish in coconut), with vegetarian options. Reservations are advised.

## ESPERANÇA

Rua do Norte 95 ☎ 213 432 027. Daily noon–3pm & 7.30pm–midnight. MAP P.62–63, POCKET MAP C11

Fashionable and jazzy haunt for mid-priced Italian dishes including filling pasta dishes, fine risottos and decent pizzas, all from around €9.

## ESPLANADA

Praça do Príncipe Real ☎ 962 311 669. Daily 8am–11pm. MAP P.62–63, POCKET MAP A10

A good range of quiches and chunky sandwiches makes this an ideal and inexpensive lunch spot. The outdoor tables set under the trees get snapped up quickly, though the glass

LA PAPARRUCHA

pavilion comes into its own when the weather turns. It's also a popular gay haunt.

## FAZ FRIO

Rua Dom Pedro V 96–98 ☎ 213 461 860. Daily 9am–midnight; usually closed late Aug–late Sept. MAP P.62–63, POCKET MAP B10

A traditional restaurant, replete with coloured tiles and confessional-like cubicles. The huge portions of *bacalhau*, seafood paella and prawns in breadcrumbs are good value, as are a variety of dishes of the day. Mains €9–10.

## GÁVEAS

Rua das Gáveas 82–84 ☎ 213 426 460. Mon–Fri noon–3pm & 7.30–11.30pm, Sat 7.30–11.30pm. MAP P.62–63, POCKET MAP C11

Good-value if spartan *adega* (wine cellar) with reliable dishes of the day and a long menu featuring pasta, *açorda*, meats and *bacalhau*. Mains around €9–10.

## LOURO E SAL

Rua da Atalaia 53 ☎213 476 275. Daily except Tuesday 7pm–12.30am. MAP P.62–63, POCKET MAP B12

Typical of a new breed of fashionable restaurants in the area, offering good-value nouveau Portuguese cuisine such as tuna in pastry and salmon with capers, with mains from around €10.

## PAP'AÇORDA

Rua da Atalaia 57–59 ☎ 213 464 811. Tues–Sat 12.30–2pm & 8–11.30pm. MAP P.62–63, POCKET MAP B11

Renowned restaurant that attracts Lisbon's fashionable elite to its chandelier-hung dining room. *Açorda* is the house speciality There are also regional dishes (including mixed fish with aleoli) and fine starters such as oysters or tiger prawns. Mains start at €17. Reservations are advised.

## LA PAPARRUCHA

Rua Dom Pedro V 18–20 ☎ 213 425 333.
Mon–Fri noon–3pm & 7pm–2am, Sat & Sun
1–4pm & 7pm–2am. MAP P.62-63, POCKET MAP B10

The best feature of this Argentinian restaurant is the fantastic
back room and terrace offering
superb views over the Baixa.
The food is recommended too,
especially if you like steaks,
though the fish, pasta and
vegetarian options are also
great. Mains from €14, with
good-value lunchtime buffets
from around €10.

## SINAL VERMELHO

Rua das Gáveas 89 ☎ 213 461 252. Mon–Sat
12.30–2.30pm & 7.30–11.30pm; closed July.
MAP P.62-63, POCKET MAP C11

Roomy *adega* (wine cellar)
that's popular with Lisbon's
moneyed youth. Specialities
(€10–14) include well-presented
*açorda de gambas* (prawns in
garlicky bread sauce) and *arroz
de polvo* (octopus rice), and
there's an impressive wine list.
It is best to book ahead.

## SUL

Rua do Norte 13 ☎ 213 462 449. Tues–Sat
noon–2am, Sun–Mon 7pm–midnight. MAP
P.62-63, POCKET MAP C12

Jazzy, split-level wine bar and
restaurant – the round table in
the lower mezzanine is ideal
for groups. Dishes include
chicken kebabs, risotto and *bife
na pedra* (steak cooked on a
stone). Mains from €17.

## TASCA DO MANEL

Rua da Barroca 24 ☎ 213 463 813. Mon–Sat
noon–3pm & 7.30–11pm. MAP P.62-63, POCKET
MAP C12

One of the dying breed of
inexpensive *tascas* in this
district, still attracting a largely
local crowd for wholesome
dishes such as wild boar,
grilled salmon or squid from
around €10.

TERRA

## TASCARDOSO

Rua Dom Pedro V 137 ☎ 213 427 578. Mon–
Sat noon–3pm & 7pm–midnight. MAP P.62-63,
POCKET MAP A10

Go through the stand-up bar
and down the stairs to the tiny
eating area for excellent and
inexpensive tapas-style meats
and cheeses and good-value
hot dishes from around €7.

## TERRA

Rua da Palmeira 15 ☎ 707 108 108. Daily
12.30–3.30pm & 7.30–10.30pm. MAP P.62-63,
POCKET MAP A10

Attractive vegetarian and vegan
restaurant with a lovely patio
garden and well-priced salads
and pasta dishes. The all-you-
can-eat buffets are good value
at around €15; leave room for
the Italian ice creams.

# Cafés

## CATEDRAL DO PÃO

Rua Dom Pedro V 57c. Daily 7am–7pm. MAP
P.62-63, POCKET MAP B10

Relaxed corner café-bakery
with a wonderfully ornate high
ceiling. You can have coffee and
croissants at the counter or buy
fresh pastries to take away.

CLUBE DA ESQUINA

### PÃO DE CANELA

Praça das Flôres 27–28. Mon–Fri
7.30am–11pm, Sat & Sun 8am–11pm. MAP
P.62-63, POCKET MAP H6

Tastefully modernized, tile-
fronted café serving great
pastries, soups and snacks.
The outdoor terrace faces a
children's play area on this
lovely square.

### TEASE

Rua do Norte 31–33. Daily noon–11pm. MAP
P.62-63, POCKET MAP C12

Unusual for this part of town,
this café-cum-bar has soft
velvet sofas to slump in while
you sip herbal teas, infusions or
delicious cupcakes – or if you
fancy something stronger, a
fruit cocktail.

# Bars and clubs

### ARROZ DOCE

Rua da Atalaia 117–119 ☎ 213 462 601.
Mon–Sat 6pm–4am. MAP P.62-63, POCKET MAP B11

An unpretentious bar in the
middle of the frenetic Bairro
Alto, with friendly owners;
try "Auntie's" sangria and the
evening will never be the same.

### BAR ÁRTIS

Rua do Diário de Notícias 95 ☎ 213 424
795. Tues–Fri 7.30pm–2am, Sat & Sun
7.30pm–4am. MAP P.62-63, POCKET MAP B11

A fashionable tapas bar – a
good place to sample local
wines while tapas (€3.30–6)
includes tasty pork with
coriander and garlic, local
cheeses and spicy *chouriço*.

### BEDROOM BAR

Rua do Norte 86 ☎ 213 431 631. Mon–Sat
10pm–3am. MAP P.62-63, POCKET MAP C11

This large, flash space has
taken the lounge bar concept a
step further by installing beds
where you can chill out with a
cocktail – though the pulsing
music keeps most of the action
away from the sheets.

### CINCO LOUNGE

Rua Ruben A. Leitão 179. Tues–Sat
9pm–2am. MAP P.62-63, POCKET MAP A11

A New York-style cocktail
lounge run by Brits in the heart
of Lisbon – there are over a
hundred cocktails to choose
from; go for one of the wacky
fruit concoctions (anyone
for hazelnut and vanilla?)
while sinking into one of the
enormous comfy sofas.

### CLUBE DA ESQUINA

Rua da Barroca 30 ☎ 213 427 149. Daily
4.30pm–2am. MAP P.62-63, POCKET MAP B12

Buzzing little corner bar with
ancient radios on the walls and
DJs spinning discs. Attracts
a young crowd enjoying vast
measures of spirits.

### ENOTECA

Rua da Mãe de Agua ☎ 213 422 079. Tues–
Sun 6pm–2am. MAP P.62-63, POCKET MAP B10

This extraordinary wine
bar is set in the bowels of a
nineteenth-century bathhouse
whose underground tunnels
once piped water into Lisbon.
The bar offers a long list of

Portuguese wines, which you can enjoy with regional breads and assorted *petiscos* (snacks) such as oysters or dates with bacon. It gets busy at weekends so it's best to reserve if you want to eat, though you can always squeeze in for a drink or sit at one of the outside tables.

### FINALMENTE

Rua da Palmeira 38 ☎ 213 479 923. Daily 11am–6am. MAP P.62-63, POCKET MAP A10

A gay disco with lashings of kitsch, famed for its drag shows (at 2am) featuring skimpily dressed "*senhoritas*" camping it up to high-tech sounds.

### FRÁGIL

Rua da Atalaia 126 ☎ 213 469 578, ⓦ www .fragil.com. Mon–Sat 11pm–4am. MAP P.62-63, POCKET MAP B11

This has long been one of Lisbon's most popular clubs, and it remains very lively, particularly from Thursday to Saturday, though it doesn't really get going until after 1am. It's wonderfully pretentious and has a strict door policy (it helps if you're young and beautiful). You'll need to ring the bell to get in.

### JANELA DA ATALAIA

Rua da Atalaia 160 ☎ 213 465 988. Mon–Sat 9pm–4am. MAP P.62-63, POCKET MAP B11

A fine old bar with two rooms, inexpensive drinks and laid-back sounds, usually world music. Most Wednesdays there's a band, often salsa/ Brazilian.

### LISBONA

Rua da Atalaia 196 ☎ 213 471 412. Mon–Sat 7pm–2am. MAP P.00 POCKET MAP B11

Earthy bar attracting its fair share of local characters and Bairro Alto trendies. Decor is basic – chequerboard tiles covered in soccer memorabilia, old film posters and graffiti –

but there's catchy pop music and good beer.

### MAJONG

Rua da Atalaia 3 ☎ 213 421 039. Daily 7pm–2am. MAP P.62-63, POCKET MAP B12

At the bottom of the Bairro Alto and traditionally a place to start an evening before moving on up. It's a great space, with plain white tiles and a rough wooden bar juxtaposed with modern Chinese motifs – the clientele are similarly eclectic.

### PAVILHÃO CHINÊS

Rua Dom Pedro V 89 ☎ 213 424 729. Mon–Sat 6pm–2am, Sun 9pm–2am. MAP P.62-63, POCKET MAP B10

Once a nineteenth-century tea and coffee merchants' shop, this is now a quirky bar set in a series of comfy rooms, including a pool room. Most are completely lined with mirrored cabinets containing a bizarre range of artefacts from around the world, including a cabinet of model trams. There's waiter service and the usual drinks are supplemented by a long list of exotic cocktails.

BAIRRO ALTO

## PORTAS LARGAS

Rua da Atalaia 105 ☎ 218 466 379. Daily 8pm–4am. MAP P.62-63, POCKET MAP B11

The bar's *portas largas* (big doors) are usually thrown wide open, inviting the neighbourhood into this friendly black-and-white-tiled *adega* (wine cellar). There are cheapish drinks, music from fado to pop, and a young, mixed gay and straight clientele, which spills onto the streets on warm evenings before hitting *Frágil*, just over the road.

## SÉTIMO CÉU

Trav. da Espera 54 ☎ 213 466 471. Mon–Sat 10pm–2am. MAP P.62-63, POCKET MAP B12

An obligatory stop for gays and lesbians, who imbibe beers and *caipirinhas* served by the Brazilian owner. The great atmosphere spills out onto the street.

## SOLAR DO VINHO DO PORTO

Rua de São Pedro de Alcântara 45 ☎ 213 475 707. Ⓦ www.ivp.pt. Mon–Sat 11am–midnight. MAP P.62-63, POCKET MAP B11

The Port Wine Institute is set in the eighteenth-century Palácio Ludovice. The Institute, based in the northern city of Porto, regulates and promotes the production of port wine. It opened its Lisbon headquarters here in 1944 and now lures in visitors with over three hundred types of port, starting at around €3 a glass and rising to some €30 for a glass of forty-year-old J.W. Burmester. Drinks are served at low tables in a comfortable old eighteenth-century mansion. The waiters are notoriously snooty and the cheaper ports never seem to be in stock, but it's still a good place to kick off an evening.

## SNOB

Rua do Século 178 ☎ 213 463 723. Daily 4.30pm–3am. MAP P.62-63, POCKET MAP A10

Cosy and upmarket bar and restaurant, full of media types enjoying cocktails. It's a good late-night option which also serves inexpensive steaks or light snacks.

## A TASCA TEQUILA BAR

Trav. da Queimada 13–15. Daily 11.30am–2am. MAP P.62-63, POCKET MAP C11

Colourful Mexican bar with

SOLAR DO VINHO DO PORTO

Latin sounds, which caters to a good-time crowd downing tequilas, margaritas and Brazilian *caipirinhas*.

## TRUMPS

Rua da Imprensa Nacional 104b ☎ 213 971 059. Tues–Sun 11.30pm–6am. MAP P.62-63, POCKET MAP H5

Popular gay disco with a reasonably relaxed door policy. It's a bit cruisy during the middle of the week, and it gets packed from Thursday to Saturday, when there's also a high lesbian turnout. Drag shows are held on Wednesdays and Sundays.

## ZÉ DOS BOIS

Rua da Barroca 59 ☎ 213 430 205, ⓦ www.zedebois.org. Fri & Sat 11pm–2am. MAP P.62-63, POCKET MAP B12

Rambling arts venue that hosts installations, films and exhibitions (hours vary – phone for details) along with occasional concerts. At weekends, local DJs showcase their talents to a bohemian crowd.

# Fado

## ADEGA MACHADO

Rua do Norte 91 ☎ 213 224 640. Tues–Sun 8.30pm–3am. MAP P.62-63, POCKET MAP C11

Beautiful music-themed tiles mark the entrance to one of the longest-established Bairro Alto fado houses, offering fado from both Lisbon and Coimbra. A minimum charge of €16 builds to at least €30 a head if you sample the fine Portuguese cooking.

## ADEGA DO RIBATEJO

Rua do Diário de Notícias 23 ☎ 213 468 343. Mon–Sat noon–midnight. MAP P.62-63, POCKET MAP B12

This great little *adega* (wine cellar) is a favoured haunt for British artists Gilbert and

PORTUGUESE GUITAR

George. It's popular with locals, too, who describe the fado (from 8.30pm nightly) here as "pure emotion". The singers include a couple of professionals, the manager and – best of all – the cooks. Also has one of the lowest minimum charges (around €15) and delicious, inexpensive food.

## A SEVERA

Rua das Gáveas 51–61 ☎ 213 428 314, ⓦ www.asevera.com. Mon–Tues & Thurs–Sun 8pm–3am. MAP P.62-63, POCKET MAP C12

A city institution, named after the nineteenth-century singer Maria Severa. The club attracts big fado names and equally large prices. Minimum consumption of €20 builds to more like €40 with food (served until midnight).

## TASCA DO CHICO

Rua do Diário de Notícias ☎ 213 431 040. Daily 8pm–midnight. MAP P.62-63, POCKET MAP B12

Atmospheric little bar (a fine spot for a drink) which morphs into a very popular fado bar from Mon–Wed, when crowds pack in to hear moving fado from 8pm.

# Estrela, Lapa and Santos

West of the Bairro Alto sits the leafy district of Estrela, best known for its gardens and enormous basilica. To the south lies opulent Lapa, Lisbon's diplomatic quarter, sheltering some of its top hotels. Sumptuous mansions and grand embassy buildings peer out majestically towards the Tejo. The superb Museu Nacional de Arte Antiga below here is Portugal's national gallery, while down on the riverfront, Santos is being promoted as "the district of design" with some of the city's coolest shops and bars along with some long-established clubs.

## BASÍLICA AND JARDIM DA ESTRELA

Basílica daily 8am–8pm. Free. Tram #28 or 25.
MAP OPPOSITE, POCKET MAP G6

The impressive Basílica da Estrela is a vast monument to late eighteenth-century Neoclassicism. Constructed by order of Queen Maria I (whose tomb lies within), and completed in 1790, its landmark white dome can be seen from much of the city. Opposite is the **Jardim da Estrela** (daily, free), one of the city's most enjoyable gardens; it is a quiet refuge with a pond-side café, a well-equipped children's playground and even a library kiosk for those who fancy sampling Portuguese literature under the palms.

## CEMITÉRIO DOS INGLESES

Tram #28 or 25. MAP OPPOSITE, POCKET MAP G6

The name translates as "The English Cemetery" (ring the bell loudly for entry) but it is actually a cemetery for all Protestants, founded in 1717. Here, among the cypresses and tombs of various expatriates, lie the remains of Henry Fielding, author of *Tom Jones*. He came to Lisbon hoping the climate would improve his failing health, but his inability to recuperate may have influenced his verdict on Lisbon as "the nastiest city in the world".

BASÍLICA DA ESTRELA

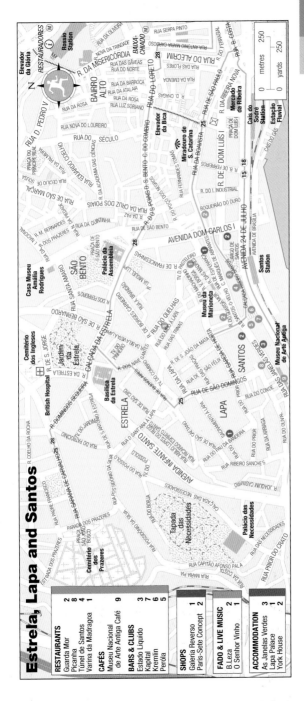

# Estrela, Lapa and Santos

**RESTAURANTS**
Guarda Mor          2
Picanha             8
Tunel de Santos     4
Varina da Madragoa  1

**CAFÉS**
Museu Nacional
de Arte Antiga Café  9

**BARS & CLUBS**
Estado Líquido   3
Kapital          7
Kremlin          6
Pérola           5

**SHOPS**
Galeria Reverso      1
Paris-Sete Concept   2

**FADO & LIVE MUSIC**
B.Leza           2
O Senhor Vinho   1

**ACCOMMODATION**
As Janelas Verdes   3
Lapa Palace         1
York House          2

## LAPA

MAP P.75, POCKET MAP F7

From Estrela tram 25# skirts past the well-heeled district of Lapa on its way down to the waterfront. Lapa is the most desired address in the city and though it contains no sights as such, it is worth wandering around to admire the stunning mansions. A good route is to follow the tram tracks from Estrela and turn right into Rua do Sacramento à Lapa, past fantastic embassy buildings. Turn left into Rua do Pau da Bandeira past the plush *Lapa Palace* hotel (if you have the funds, you can have a drink at the bar). From here, go left into Rua do Prior and right into Rua do Conde and it's a ten-minute walk downhill to the Museu Nacional de Arte Antiga (see below).

## MUSEU NACIONAL DE ARTE ANTIGA

Rua das Janelas Verdes 95 ☎ 213 912 800. Ⓦ www.mnarteantiga-ipmuseus.pt. Tues 2–6pm, Wed–Sun 10am–6pm. €4, free Sun 10am–2pm. Bus #60, #713 or #727 or a short walk from tram #25. MAP P.75, POCKET MAP G8

The Museu Nacional de Arte Antiga features the largest collection of Portuguese fifteenth- and sixteenth-century paintings in the country, European art from the fourteenth century to the present day and a rich display of applied art. All of this is well exhibited in a tastefully converted seventeenth-century palace once owned by the Marquês de Pombal. The museum uses ten "reference points" to guide you round the collection. The principal highlight is **Nuno Gonçalves's altarpiece** dedicated to St Vincent (1467–70), a brilliantly marshalled composition depicting Lisbon's patron saint receiving homage from all ranks of its citizens, their faces appearing remarkably modern. The other main highlight is Hieronymus Bosch's stunningly gruesome *Temptation of St Anthony* in room 57 (don't miss the image on the back of the painting, showing the arrest of Christ). Elsewhere, seek out the altar panel depicting the *Resurrection* by Raphael; Francisco de Zurbarán's *The Twelve Apostles;* a small statue of a nymph by Auguste Rodin and works by Albrecht Dürer, Holbein, Cranach (particularly

*Salome*), Fragonard and Josefa de Óbidos, considered one of Portugal's greatest female painters.

The **Oriental art** collection shows how the Portuguese were influenced by overseas designs encountered during the sixteenth century. There is inlaid furniture from Goa, Turkish and Syrian azulejos, Qing Dynasty porcelain and a fantastic series of late sixteenth-century Japanese *namban* screens (room 14), depicting the Portuguese landing at Nagasaki. The Japanese regarded the Portuguese traders as southern barbarians (*namban*) with large noses – hence their Pinocchio-like features. The museum extends over the remains of the sixteenth-century St Albert monastery, most of which was razed during the 1755 earthquake, although its beautiful chapel can still be seen today, downstairs by the main entrance. Don't miss the garden café, either (see p.78).

SANTOS DISTRICT

## MUSEU DA MARIONETA

Rua da Esperança 146 ☎ 213 942 810. Tues–Sun 10am–1pm & 2–6pm. €3 (children €2). Tram #25 then a short walk. MAP P.75, POCKET MAP G7

Contemporary and historical puppets from around the world are displayed in this former eighteenth-century convent and demonstrated in a well-laid-out museum. Highlights include shadow puppets from Turkey and Indonesia, string marionettes, Punch and Judy-style puppets and almost life-sized, faintly disturbing modern figures by Portuguese puppeteer Helena Vaz, which are anything but cute. There are also video displays and projections, while the final room exhibits Wallace and Gromit-style plasticine figures with demonstrations on how they are manipulated for films.

## SANTOS

MAP P.75, POCKET MAP G7

Santos was traditionally a run-down riverside area of factories and warehouses where people only ventured after dark because of its nightclubs. Over the years, artists and designers moved into the inexpensive and expansive warehouse spaces, and now Santos has a reputation as the city's designer heartland. Its riverside streets are not particularly alluring, but you can see many of the country's top designers showcasing their products in various shops and galleries – the last Thursday of each month has an open day with exhibitions and street entertainment. Fashionable bars and restaurants have followed in their wake, though much of the upper district remains fairly traditional – and the area around the Museu da Marioneta retains an earthy, villagey feel to its cobbled backstreets.

# Shops

### GALERIA REVERSO

Rua da Esperança 59–61 ☎ 213 951 407.
Mon–Sat 2–7pm. MAP P.75, POCKET MAP H7

Jewellery workshop and gallery
managed by well-known
Portuguese designer Paula
Crespo, whose big, heavy
jewellery is eye-catching.
International designers also
feature, many using unusual
materials such as rubber and
wood, though to buy anything
you'll need a deep purse.

### PARIS-SETE CONCEPT

Largo V. Damásio 2a/b. Mon–Fri
10am–7.30pm, Sat 10.30am–noon & 1–7pm.
MAP P.75, POCKET MAP H7

Bright, white space selling
designer kitchenware, bins,
toys and curios, with heavy-
weight names such as Charles
and Ray Eames and Frank
Gehry behind some of them.
*Paris Sete* at #14d Largo de
Santos focuses on furniture
and larger household items.

# Restaurants

### GUARDA MOR

Rua do Guara Mor 8 ☎ 213 928 663.
Tues–Fri 12.30–3pm & 7.30–11pm, Sat & Sun
7.30–11pm. MAP P.75, POCKET MAP G7

One of Santos' more local
options serving great, inexpensive dishes such as *pataniscas
de bacalhau* (dried cod cakes),
*açorda de gambas* (prawns in
bread sauce) and *gambas fritas
com limão* (prawns fried in
lemon). Mains from €10.

### PICANHA

Rua das Janelas Verdes 96 ☎ 213 658 300.
Mon–Fri 12.45–3pm & 7.45–11.30pm, Sat &
Sun 7.45–11.30pm. MAP P.75, POCKET MAP G8

This ornately tiled restaurant
specializes in *picanha* (strips of
beef in garlic sauce) accompanied by black-eyed beans,
salad and potatoes. Great if
this appeals to you, since for a
fixed-price of around €15 you
can eat as much of the stuff as
you want; otherwise forget it, as
it's all that's on offer.

### TÚNEL DE SANTOS

Largo de Santos 1 ☎ 912 151 850. Mon–Sun
8am–10pm. MAP P.75, POCKET MAP G7

Lively, modern café-restaurant
with brick-vaulted ceilings
and outdoor seating facing
the square, attracting a young
crowd for inexpensive grills,
snacks and salads.

### VARINA DA MADRAGOA

Rua das Madres 34 ☎ 213 965 533. Tues–Fri
12.45–3.30pm & 7.45–11.30pm, Sat
7.45–11.30pm. MAP P.75, POCKET MAP G7

A delightfully simple local that
has hosted the likes of fomer
US President Jimmy Carter and
Portuguese PM José Socrates
– and it's easy to see why they
liked it: a lovely, traditional
restaurant with grape-motif
azulejos on the walls and a
menu featuring dishes such
as *bacalhau*, trout and steaks.
Desserts include a splendid
almond ice cream with hot
chocolate sauce. Around €25
for a full meal.

# Cafés

### MUSEU NACIONAL DE ARTE ANTIGA CAFÉ

Rua das Janelas Verdes 95 ☎ 213 912 800,
Tues 2–6pm, Wed–Sun 10am–6pm. MAP P.75,
POCKET MAP G8

There's no need to visit the
museum to use its fantastic café
– go in through the museum
exit opposite Largo Dr J de
Figueiredo and head to the
basement. Lunches and drinks
can be enjoyed in a superb
garden studded with statues
and overlooking Lisbon's docks.

# Bars and clubs

## ESTADO LIQUIDO

Largo de Santos 4A ☎ 213 972 022, ⓦ www
.estadoliquido.com. Sun–Thurs 8pm–2am, Fri
& Sat 8pm–4am. MAP P.75, POCKET MAP G7

Right on Santos' main square,
this sushi-restaurant with
attached bar/club has a roomy
feel despite its popularity with
the kids lured by the prominent
club DJs. Easy-going door
policy and efficient service.

## KAPITAL

Avda 24 de Julho 68 ☎ 213 957 101, ⓦ www
.grupo-k.pt. Tues–Sat 11pm–6am. MAP P.75,
POCKET MAP G8

Long-established venue, with
three sleekly designed floors
full of bright young things
buying expensive drinks and
dancing to techno. It can be
hard work getting past the
style police on the door but
there's a great rooftop terrace
once you're in.

## KREMLIN

Escadinhas da Praia 5 ☎ 213 957101, ⓦ www
.grupo-k.pt. Tues–Sat midnight–8am. MAP P.75,
POCKET MAP G7

The tough door policy, based
on its reputation as one of
the city's most fashionable
nightspots, has put off many
old-hand clubbers. However,
it's still packed with flash,
young, raving Lisboetas. It's
best to come after 2am.

## PERÓLA

Calçada Ribeiro de Santos 25 ☎ 966 439
164. Mon–Sat 8am–10pm. MAP P.75, POCKET
MAP G7

A small local bar given a
fashionable makeover, with
table football to play and a little
back dining area. Most hole up
in the front room for inexpensive drinks and good music
before moving on to nearby
*Kapital* or *Kremlin*.

KREMLIN

# Fado and live music

## B.LEZA

Largo Conde de Barão 50 ☎ 213 963 735.
Wed–Sat 11.30pm–4am. MAP P.75, POCKET
MAP H7

There's live African music
most nights in this wonderful
sixteenth-century building,
with plenty of space to dance,
tables to relax at, and Cape
Verdean food.

## O SENHOR VINHO

Rua do Meio à Lapa 18 ☎ 213 972 681,
ⓦ www.srvinho.com. Mon–Sat 7.30pm–2am.
MAP P.75, POCKET MAP G7

In the fashionable Madragoa
district, this famous fado
club features some of the best
singers in Portugal, hence the
high prices (usually around
€50 a head). Reservations are
advised, and remember – it's
simply not done to talk during
a performance!

# Alcântara and the docks

Loomed over by the enormous Ponte 25 de Abril suspension bridge, Alcântara has a decidedly industrial hue, with a tangle of flyovers and cranes from the docks dominating the skyline. This is where cruise ships unload their passengers, at least until a new terminal is completed. The area is well known for its nightlife, thanks mainly to its dockside warehouse conversions that shelter cafés, restaurants and clubs. It also hosts a couple of fine museums, both tipping their hats to Portugal's historic links with the Far East. To get to the docks, take a train from Cais do Sodré to Alcântara-Mar or tram #15.

## DOCA DE ALCÂNTARA

MAP BELOW, POCKET MAP F8

The earthy Doca de Alcântara remains the city's main docks with giant luxury cruise ships calling frequently. After dark, the boat-bars and warehouse conversions come into their own; its clubs and bars attract an older, more moneyed crowd compared to the Bairro Alto set who wouldn't be seen dead in these parts.

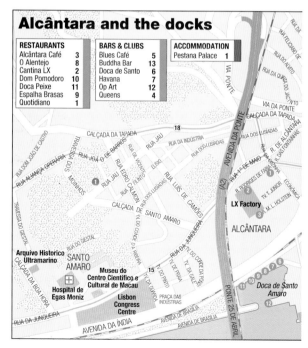

**Alcântara and the docks**

| RESTAURANTS | | BARS & CLUBS | | ACCOMMODATION | |
|---|---|---|---|---|---|
| Alcântara Café | 3 | Blues Café | 5 | Pestana Palace | 1 |
| O Alentejo | 8 | Buddha Bar | 13 | | |
| Cantina LX | 2 | Doca de Santo | 6 | | |
| Dom Pomodoro | 10 | Havana | 7 | | |
| Doca Peixe | 11 | Op Art | 12 | | |
| Espalha Brasas | 9 | Queens | 4 | | |
| Quotidiano | 1 | | | | |

## MUSEU DO ORIENTE

Avenida Brasília ☎ 213 585 200, Ⓦ www
.museudooriente.pt. Wed–Sun 10am–6pm,
late opening Fri until 10pm. €4, free Fri
6–10pm. MAP BELOW, POCKET MAP E8

MUSEU DO ORIENTE

Owned by the powerful Orient Foundation, this spacious museum traces the cultural links that Portugal has built up with its former colonies in Macao, India, East Timor and other Asian countries. Housed in an enormous 1930s *Estado Novo* building, highlights of the extensive collection include valuable nineteenth-century Chinese porcelain, an amazing array of seventeenth-century Chinese snuff boxes and, from the same century, Japanese armour and entire carved pillars from Goa. The top floor is given over to displays on the Gods of Asia, featuring a bright collection of religious costumes and shrines used in Bali and Vietnam together with Taoist altars, statues of Buddha, some fine Japanese Shinto masks and Indonesian shadow puppets. Vivid images of Hindu gods Shiva, Ganesh the elephant god and Kali the demon are counterbalanced by some lovely Thai amulets. There is also a decent top-floor restaurant.

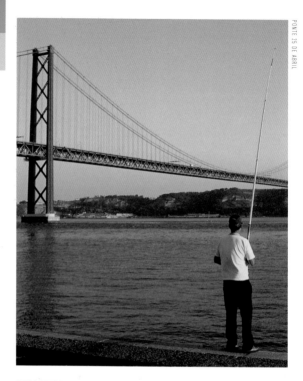

PONTE 25 DE ABRIL

## DOCA DE SANTO AMARO

MAP P.80-81, POCKET MAP D9

Just west of the Doca de Alcântara lies the more intimate
Doca de Santo Amaro, nestling
right under the humming
traffic and rattling trains
crossing Ponte 25 de Abril.
This small, almost completely
enclosed marina is filled with
bobbing sailing boats and
lined with tastefully converted
warehouses. Its international
cafés and restaurants are
pricier than usual for Lisbon
but the constant comings and
goings of the Tejo provide
plenty of free entertainment.
Leaving Doca de Santo Amaro
at its western side, you can
pick up a pleasant riverside
path that leads all the way
to Belém (see p.86), twenty
minutes' walk away.

## PONTE 25 DE ABRIL

MAP P.80-81, POCKET MAP D9

Resembling the Golden Gate
bridge in San Francisco, the
hugely impressive Ponte 25
de Abril was opened in 1966
as a vital link between Lisbon
and the southern banks of the
Tejo. Around 2.3km in length,
the main bridge rises to 70m
above the river, though its
main pillars are nearly 200m
tall. It was originally named
Ponte de Salazar after the
dictatorial prime minister
who ruled Portugal with an
iron fist from 1932 to 1968,
but took its present name to
mark the date of the revolution that overthrew Salazar's
regime in 1974. You'll pass
over it if you take a bus or train
south of the Tejo. Driving over
it is pretty hairy, especially

on the lane made up of wire mesh (it allows the bridge to expand) – it is both skiddy and see-through.

## MUSEU DO CENTRO CIENTÍFICO E CULTURAL DE MACAU

Rua da Junqueira 30 ☎ 213 617 570, Ⓦ www .cccm.mctes.pt. Tues–Sun 10am–6pm. €3.50, free Sun 10am–2pm. MAP P.80-81, POCKET MAP C9

This attractively laid-out museum is dedicated to Portugal's historical trading links with the Orient and, specifically, its former colony of Macao, which was handed back to Chinese rule in 1999. There are model boats and audio displays detailing early sea voyages, as well as various historic journals and artefacts, including a seventeenth-century portable wooden altar, used by travelling clergymen. Upstairs, exhibitions of Chinese art from the sixteenth to the nineteenth centuries show off ornate collections of porcelain, silverware and applied art, most notably an impressive array of opium pipes and ivory boxes.

## LX FACTORY

Rua Rodrigues Faria 103 Ⓦ www.lxfactory .com. MAP P.80-81, POCKET MAP D8

LER DEVAGAR, LX FACTORY

Below Ponte 25 de Abril, this former industrial estate is now the place to test Lisbon's creative pulse. The factories and warehouses have turned into a mini district of workshops and studios for the city's go-getters, along with a series of superb boutiques and cafés set in fashionably run-down urban spaces. Highlights include *Ler Devagar*, a bookshop with shelves reaching to the heavens of an old printing press and complete with its own café-bar and exhibition space; and *Cantina LX* (see p.84). Check the website for LX Factory's Open Days, when there are shows, live music and film screenings.

## Ethnic Lisbon

When Africans sailed on the Tejo in the fifteenth century, most would have first glimpsed Lisbon as they passed Alcântara on slave ships during Portugal's ruthless maritime explorations. Today, over 120,000 people of African and Asian descent live in the Greater Lisbon area, most hailing originally from Portugal's former colonies – Cape Verde, Angola, Mozambique, Brazil, Goa and Macao. The 1974 revolution and subsequent independence of the former colonies saw another wave of immigrants settle in the capital. Nowadays African and Brazilian culture permeate Lisbon life, influencing its music, food, television and street slang. Most Lisboetas are rightly proud of their cosmopolitan city, although, inevitably, racism persists and few from ethnic minorities have managed to break through the glass ceiling to the top jobs.

DOM POMODORO

# Restaurants

### ALCÂNTARA CAFÉ

Rua Maria Luísa Holstein 15 ☎ 213 637 176.
Daily 8pm–3am. MAP P.80–81, POCKET MAP D8
Stunning, if pricey, designer
bar-restaurant, blending
industrial steel pillars with
stylish decor. The food on
offer includes prawns in lemon
sauce, goat's cheese salad and
an array of fish dishes. Reservations advised.

### O ALENTEJO

Pavilhão 1, Doca de Santo Amaro ☎ 213
908 024. Daily noon–midnight. MAP P.80–81,
POCKET MAP D9
Named after the southern
Portuguese region, specialities
include its fine mixed sausages
and *carne de porco alentejano*
(pork with clams). Mains from
€15 but high quality.

### CANTINA LX

Rua Rodrigues Faria 103 ☎ 213 628 239.
Mon–Sat 9am–9pm. MAP P.80–81, POCKET MAP D8
This is the place to be seen in
the LX Factory complex (see
p.83), with bench-like tables in
a spacious former warehouse.
Great breakfasts, snacks and
daily specials which usually
focus on healthy salads from
around €8.

### DOM POMODORO

Armazém 13, Doca de Santo Amaro ☎ 213
909 353. Daily noon–2am. MAP P.80–81, POCKET
MAP D9
The best place to get an
inexpensive meal in the docks,
albeit Italian, with good-value
and tasty pasta, pizza and the
like from €9. Attractive seating
on two floors and outdoor
waterside tables.

### DOCA PEIXE

Armazém 14, Doca de Santo Amaro ☎ 213
973 556. Daily 12.30pm–11.30pm. MAP P.80–81,
POCKET MAP D9
You'll need a deep wallet to eat
at this fish restaurant, but with
a counter groaning under the
weight of fresh fish, you won't
leave disappointed. They also
serve a great fish curry and
sublime tiger prawns.

### ESPALHA BRASAS

Armazém 12, Doca de Santo Amaro ☎ 213
962 059. Mon–Sat noon–4am. MAP P.80–81,
POCKET MAP D9
Superb grilled meats, tiger
prawns and fish kebabs can be
enjoyed at the riverside tables,
or head for the bright upstairs
room, which offers great views
over the river. Daily specials
around €14.

### QUOTIDIANO

Largo das Fontainhas 7. Mon–Fri 9am–2am,
Sat & Sun 10am–1am. MAP P.80–81, POCKET
MAP D8
Modern and alluring café-
restaurant on a lively square,
serving a range of quality cakes,
pastries, drinks and reasonably
priced dishes of the day (under
€9); packed at lunchtime so
arrive early.

# Bars and clubs

## BLUES CAFÉ

Rua da Cintura do Porto de Lisboa ☎ 213 957 085. Tues–Thurs 8pm–4am, Fri & Sat 8pm–5am. MAP P.80–81, POCKET MAP F8

Lisbon's only blues club occupies a converted dockside warehouse. There's pricey Cajun food served in the restaurant until 12.30am, live music on Mondays and Thursdays, and club nights with the latest dance music on Fridays and Saturdays from 2.30am.

## BUDDHA BAR

Gare Marítima de Alcântara ☎ 213 950 555, Ⓦ www.buddha.com.pt. Tues–Thurs 10pm–4am, Fri & Sat 10pm–6am. MAP P.80–81, POCKET MAP E9

Wonderful Eastern-influenced bar and club housed in a 1940s maritime station, inspired by the Paris original. There are many chillout areas upstairs, most with an "opium den" feel, with a big dancefloor downstairs. Smart dress is recommended, and check opening hours in advance as it's sometimes booked for private functions.

CANTINA LX

## DOCA DE SANTO

Doca de Santo Amaro ☎ 213 963 535. Mon–Thurs 12.30pm–1am, Fri–Sun 12.30pm–4am. MAP P.80–81, POCKET MAP D8

Though it's located slightly away from the river, this palm-fringed venue is worth seeking out; there's an enticing cocktail bar on the esplanade, while the restaurant inside serves well-priced modern Portuguese food (grilled fish and meats with pasta or couscous).

## HAVANA

Armazém 5, Doca de Santo Amaro ☎ 213 979 893, Ⓦ www.havana.com.pt. Daily noon–6am. MAP P.80–81, POCKET MAP D9

Cuban-themed music bar with wicker chairs and Latin music. It also does moderately priced salads and snacks.

## OP ART

Doca de Santo Amaro ☎ 213 956 797 Ⓦ www .opartcafe.com. Tues–Fri & Sun 3pm–2am. Sat 3pm–6am. MAP P.80–81, POCKET MAP D9

Set in splendid isolation on the fringes of the Tejo, this small glass pavilion morphs from a minimalist restaurant serving moderately priced grills into a groovy evening bar. After dusk, the volume pumps up and it turns into more of a club. In summer, you can sprawl on the dockside beanbags and gaze over the river.

## QUEENS

Rua Cintura do Porto de Lisboa, Armázem H, Naves A–B ☎ 213 955 870. Tues–Sat 10pm–6am. MAP P.80 POCKET MAP F8

Launched as a "high-tech gay disco", this has since attracted a large following of beautiful people of all sexual persuasions. It's a huge, pulsating place which can hold up to 2,500 people. Tuesday night is "Ladies' Night" which involves a male strip show; there are visiting DJs on other nights.

# Belém and Ajuda

With its maritime history and attractive riverside location, Belém (pronounced ber-layng) is understandably one of Lisbon's most popular suburbs. It was from Belém that Vasco da Gama famously set sail for India in 1497 and returned a year later. The monastery subsequently built here – the Mosteiro dos Jerónimos – stands as a testament to his triumphant discovery of a sea route to the Orient, which initiated the beginning of a Portuguese golden age. Along with the monastery and the landmark Torre de Belém, the suburb boasts a group of small museums including the fantastic Berardo Collection of modern art. Just to the north-east of Belém is Ajuda, famed for its palace and ancient botanical gardens. Higher still lies the extensive parkland of Monsanto, Lisbon's largest green space.

## PRAÇA DO IMPÉRIO

MAP P.88–89, POCKET MAP C4

The formal gardens and walkways that make up Praça do Império are laid out over Belém's former beach. It's a popular spot, especially on Saturday mornings, when there are often weddings taking place at the monastery, whose photo-calls invariably spill out into the square. The attractive seventeenth-century buildings along Rua Vieira Portuense are now mostly restaurants with outdoor seating; as a rule, the further east you head, the better value they become.

## JARDIM DO ULTRAMAR AND PRESIDÊNCIA DA REPÚBLICA

Garden entrance on Calçada do Galvão. Daily May–Sept 10am–6pm, Oct–April 10am–5pm. €2. MAP P.88–89, POCKET MAP C4

The leafy Jardim do Ultramar is an oasis of hothouses, ponds and towering palms, a lovely place for a shady walk. In the southeastern corner lies the Portuguese President's official residence, the pink Presidência da República, which opens its lavish state rooms for guided visits on Saturdays (entrance on Praça Afonso de Albuquerque, 10am–5pm, €5; Ⓦ www.museu.presidencia.pt).

## Belém transport

You can reach Belém on tram #15 (signed Algés), which runs from Praça da Figueira via Praça do Comércio and Cais do Sodré (20min); watch out for pickpockets. At Belém, a road train (comboio turístico) follows a 45min circuit (Ⓦwww.caristur.pt; roughly hourly 10am–7pm, except 1pm, Oct–May same hours to 5pm; day ticket €3) from the Mosteiro dos Jerónimos to the Museu dos Coches, returning on an uphill route. You can also hire bikes (Wed–Fri 2pm–dusk, Sat and Sun 10am–4pm, €2.50/30 mins) from a kiosk just east of the Museu da Electricidade (see p.91)

MOSTEIRO DOS JERÓNIMOS

## ESTÁDIO DO RESTELO

Avenida do Restelo ☎ 213 010 461, ⓦ www
.cfbelenenses.com. MAP P.88-89, POCKET MAP B3
The attractively sited Estádio
do Restelo is home to
Belenenses soccer club, Lisbon's
third team. Belenenses has won
just one league title, back in
1946, but the stadium offers
such picturesque views over the
river that the soccer action is
almost insignificant. Top teams
(Porto, Benfica and the like)
frequently visit.

## MOSTEIRO DOS JERÓNIMOS

Praça do Império ☎ 213 620 034, ⓦ www
.mosteirojeronimos.pt. Daily: May–Sept
10am–6pm; Oct–April 10am–5pm; restricted
access on Sat mornings and during Mass.
Free. MAP P.88-89, POCKET MAP C4
A UNESCO World Heritage
site, the Mosteiro dos
Jerónimos is Portugal's most
successful achievement of
Manueline architecture.
Construction began in 1502,
the result of a vow that Dom
Manuel had made to the
Virgin that he would build a
monastery should Vasco da
Gama return successfully from
his trip to India. The design
was largely the brainchild of
Diogo de Boitaca, perhaps the
originator of the Manueline

style, and João de Castilho,
a Spaniard who took charge
of construction from around
1517. Castilho designed the
main entrance – an arch
decorated with a complex
hierarchy of figures clustered
around Henry the Navigator.
Just inside the entrance lie the
stone tombs of **Vasco da Gama**
(1468–1523) and the great poet
and recorder of the discoveries,
**Luís de Camões** (1527–70).

The breathtaking sense of
space inside the church places
it among the greatest triumphs
of European Gothic while its
rich Manueline detail provides
a deliberate contrast. The six
central columns resemble giant
palm trunks, growing both into
and from the branches of the
delicate rib-vaulting.

Equally stunning are the
beautifully vaulted **cloisters**
(€6, free Sun 10am–2pm). The
rounded corner canopies and
elegant twisting arches lend a
wave-like, undulating appearance to the whole structure,
a conceit extended by the
typically Manueline motifs of
ropes, anchors and the sea.
Round the edges of the cloisters
you can still see twelve niches
where pilgrims and sailors
stopped for confessionals.

# Belém and Ajuda

RUA DO ALTO D. DUQUE
AVENIDA DAS DESCOBERTAS
RUA GONÇALO VELHO CABRAL
RUA DE GONÇALO NUNES
AVENIDA DA ILHA DA MADEIRA
RUA TRISTÃO VAZ
RUA GONÇALVES ZARCO
R. ROSA DE SILVES
RUA PERO DE ALENQUER
RUA FERNÃO GOMES
RUA ANTÓNIO DE SALDANHA
RUA CONSTANTINO DE BRAGANÇA
R. L. CASTANHO DE ALMEIDA
R. RUI PEREIRA
RUA PERO DA COVILHÃ
AVENIDA DOM VASCO DA GAMA
PRAÇA DE GOA
PRAÇA DE ITÁLIA EANES
RUA DE ALCOLENA
RUA DOS JERÓNIMOS
RUA SOLDADOS DA INDIA
AVENIDA DO RESTELO
RUA DUARTE P. PEREIRA
RUA SÃO FRANCISCO DE ALMEIDA
PRAÇA DE DAMÃO
PRAÇA DE DIO
PRAÇA DE MALACA
RUA DOM LOURENÇO DE ALMEIDA
RUA DOM FRANCISCO
RUA SÃO FRANCISCO XAVIER
RUA DA TORRE DE BELÉM
RUA DOM CRISTÓVÃO DA GAMA
RUA DE PEDROUÇOS
RUA FERNÃO MENDES PINTO
R. DOS CORREDORES A PEDROUÇOS
RUA DA PRAIA DE PEDROUÇOS
VILA CORREIA
RUA BARTOLOMEU DIAS
AVENIDA DA INDIA
AVENIDA DA INDIA
DOCA PESCA
AVENIDA DE BRASÍLIA
DOCA DA PRINCESA
CAIS DA PRINCESA

Estádio do Restelo (Belenenses FC)
RESTELO
Ermida de São Jerónimo
Jardim Ducla Soares
Mosteiro dos Jerónimos
Planetário Calouste Gulbenkian
Museu de Arqueologia
Museu da Marinha
Berardo Collection
Centro Cultural de Belém
Underpass
Doca de Bom Sucesso
Padrão dos Descobrimentos
Torre de Belém

15

## MUSEU DE ARQUEOLOGIA

Praça do Império ☎ 213 620 000, Ⓦ www
.mnarqueologia-ipmuseus.pt.Tues-Sun
10am–6pm. €5,. MAP ABOVE, POCKET MAP C4
Housed in a neo-Manueline
extension to the monastery
added in 1850, the archeology
museum has a small section
on Egyptian antiquities dating
from 6000 BC, but concentrates
on Portuguese archeological
finds. It's a sparse collection
reprieved by coins and jewellery through the ages, and a
few fine Roman mosaics. The
museum is due to move to a
new location and be replaced
by a museum of travel in the
next few years.

## MUSEU DA MARINHA

Praça do Império ☎ 213 620 019, Ⓦ www
.museumarinha.pt. Tues-Sun: May-Sept
10am–6pm; Oct-April 10am–5pm. €4. MAP
ABOVE, POCKET MAP B4

In the west wing of the monastery extension is an absorbing
and gargantuan maritime
museum, packed not only with
models of ships, naval uniforms
and artefacts from Portugal's
oriental colonies, but also with
real vessels – among them
fishing boats and sumptuous
state barges, early seaplanes
and some ancient fire engines.

## CENTRO CULTURAL DE BELÉM

Praça do Império ☎ 213 612 400, Ⓦ www.ccb
.pt. MAP ABOVE, POCKET MAP B4
The stylish, modern, pink
marble Centro Cultural
de Belém was built to host
Lisbon's 1992 presidency of
the European Union. It's now
one of the city's main cultural
centres, containing the Berardo
Collection (see p.89) and
hosting regular photography
and art exhibitions, as well as
concerts and shows.

## BERARDO COLLECTION

Entrance via Centro Cultural de Belém, Praça do Império ☎ 213 612 400, ⓦ www .museuberardo.pt. Mon–Thurs & Sat–Sun 10am–7pm, Fri 10am–10pm. Free. MAP ABOVE, POCKET MAP B4

As impressive as Belém's historical monuments is this unique collection of modern art amassed by wealthy Madeiran Joe Berardo. You can enjoy some of the world's top modern artists, though not all of the vast collection is on display at the same time. Depending on when you visit, you may see Eric Fischl's giant panels of sunbathers; Andy Warhol's distinctive *Judy Garland*; and Chris Ofili's *Adoration of Captain Shit*, made with genuine dung. Portugal's Paula Rego is well represented – *The Past and Present* and *The Barn* are particularly strong. Francis Bacon, David Hockney and Mark Rothko also feature, along with various video artists – including Jakab Napras' extraordinary video-collage, *Babylon Planet*.

## PADRÃO DOS DESCOBRIMENTOS

Avenida de Brasília, reached via an underpass beneath the Avenida da Índia ☎213 016 228, ⓦwww.padraodescobrimentos.egeac.pt. Daily: May–Sept 10am–7pm, Oct–April 10am–6pm. €2.50. MAP P.88–89, POCKET MAP C5

The Padrão dos Descobrimentos (Monument to the Discoveries) is a 54m-high, caravel-shaped slab of concrete erected in 1960 to commemorate the 500th anniversary of the death of Henry the Navigator. A large and detailed statue of Henry appears at the head of a line of statues that feature Luís de Camões and other Portuguese heroes. Inside is a small exhibition space which often features displays on Lisbon's history – the entrance fee also includes a ride in the lift providing fine views of the Tejo and the Torre de Belém. Just in front of the monument, tourists pose on the marble pavement decorated with a map of the world charting the routes taken by the great Portuguese explorers.

TORRE DE BELÉM

## TORRE DE BELÉM

☎ 213 620 034. Tues–Sun: May–Sept 10am–6.30pm; Oct–April 10am–5pm. €4, free Sun 10am–2pm. MAP P.88–89, POCKET MAP A5

The Torre de Belém, 500m west of the monastery, was built over the last five years of Dom Manuel's reign (1515–20) to defend the mouth of the Tejo – before an earthquake shifted the river's course in 1777, the tower stood near the middle of the waters. The tower is the country's only example of a building started and completed during the Manueline era (the rest having been adaptations of earlier structures or completed in later years) and has become the favoured symbol used to promote Lisbon by the local tourist board.

Its Moorish influence is clear in the delicately arched windows and balconies. Prominent also in the decoration are two great icons of the age: Manuel's personal badge of an armillary sphere (representing the globe); and the cross of the military Order of Christ, once the Templars, who took a major role in all the Portuguese conquests. Clamber up the steep internal stairs via a series of bare rooms for great views from the top. When inside, it is also easy to imagine what it was like in the nineteenth century when it was used as a prison, notoriously by Dom Miguel (1828–34), who kept political enemies in the water-logged dungeons.

## MUSEU DOS COCHES

Praça Afonso de Albuquerque ☎ 213 610 850. ⓦ www.museudoscoches-ipmuseus.pt. Tues–Sun 10am–6pm, free Sun 10am–2pm. €4. MAP P.88–89, POCKET MAP D4

Once the home of the royal riding school, the Museu dos Coches (coach museum) was opened in 1905 and contains

MUSEU DOS COCHES

one of the largest collections of carriages and saddlery in the world – so large that a new building is being constructed opposite to display more of it. Heavily gilded and sometimes beautifully painted, the coaches date from the sixteenth to nineteenth centuries. From the same period are sedan chairs, children's buggies and a very rare sixteenth-century coach designed for King Felipe I (Spain's King Philip II).

## MUSEU DA ELECTRICIDADE

Avenida de Brasília ☎ 213 028 190. Tues–Sun 10am–6pm. Free; temporary exhibitions around €3. MAP P.86–89, POCKET MAP D4

The extraordinary red-brick Museu da Electricidade (Electricity Museum) is housed in an early twentieth-century electricity generating station. The highlights include a series of enormous generators, steam turbines and winches; it also hosts regular art and technology exhibitions. From in front of the museum, it is possible to walk the 1.5km along the lawned riverside all the way to the Doca de Santo Amaro one way, or the 1km to central Belém the other way.

## PALÁCIO DA AJUDA

Largo da Ajuda ☎ 213 620 264. Tram #18 from Praça do Comércio or bus #14 from Belém. Mon, Tues & Thurs–Sun 10am–5.30pm. €5, free Sun 10am–2pm. MAP P.86–89, POCKET MAP D2

This massive nineteenth-century palace sits on a hillside above Belém. Construction began in 1802, but was left incomplete when João VI and the royal family fled to Brazil to escape Napoleon's invading army in 1807. The original plans were therefore never fulfilled, though the completed section was used as a royal residence after João returned from exile in 1821. The crashingly taste-less decor was commissioned by the nineteenth-century royal, Dona Maria II (João's granddaughter), and gives an insight into the opulent life the royals lived. The Queen's bedroom comes complete with a polar bearskin rug, while the throne and ballroom are impressive for their sheer size and extravagance. The highly ornate banqueting hall, full of crystal chandeliers, is also breathtaking. The palace is occasionally used for classical music concerts.

PÁTEO ALFACINHA

## JARDIM BOTÂNICO DA AJUDA

Opposite the palace. Entrance on Calçada da Ajuda ⓦ www.jardimbotanicodaajuda.com. Mon, Tues & Thurs–Sun 9am–dusk. €2. MAP P.88–89, POCKET MAP C2

A classic example of formal Portuguese gardening, this is one of the city's oldest and most interesting botanical gardens. Commissioned by the Marquês de Pombal and laid out in 1768, it was owned by the royal family until the birth of the Republic in 1910, then substantially restored in the 1990s. The garden is divided into eight parts planted with plant species from around the world, all arranged around a system of terraces, statues and fountains, much of it offering lovely views over the river.

## PÁTEO ALFACINHA

Rua do Guarda Jóias 44 ☎ 213 642 171. MAP P.88–89, POCKET MAP D2

Just five minutes' walk from the Palácio da Ajuda, it is worth seeking out this highly picturesque *páteo* – a renovated cluster of traditional nineteenth-century Lisbon houses gathered round a central patio. These were common in the days when relatively humble families lived in tight-knit communities who looked after and traded with each other. Today the houses only come alive for special events and private parties, often laid on at weekends, though there is a permanent restaurant, *Sala Menina*, which does good-value grills.

## PARQUE FLORESTAL DE MONSANTO

Bus #43. MAP P.88–89, POCKET MAP E2

The extensive hillside Parque Florestal de Monsanto – home to the city's main and well-equipped campsite (ⓦ www. campings.net) – is known as "Lisbon's lungs" though its other main attraction used to be the prostitutes who worked here until the Mayor of Lisbon bought a house nearby in 2003. Suddenly the park was given a new lease of life and the hookers have since been replaced by horse-and-trap rides to its splendid viewpoints. At weekends in summer the whole area is completely traffic-free and pop concerts are often laid on, usually free of charge.

# Restaurants

### FLORESTA BELÉM

Praça Afonso de Albuquerque 1. Tues–Sat noon–4pm & 6.30pm–midnight, Sun noon–4pm. MAP P.88–89, POCKET MAP C4

On the corner with Rua Vieira Portuense, this attracts a largely Portuguese clientele, especially for lunch at the weekend. Great salads, grills and fresh fish from around €7, served inside or on a sunny outdoor terrace.

### ROTA DO INFANTE

Rua Vieira Portuense 10–14 ☎ 213 646 787. Tues–Sun noon–3pm & 7.30–11pm. MAP P.88–89, POCKET MAP C4

One of the best-value places in this pretty row of buildings facing the greenery of Praça do Império. Decently priced fish and meat from around €8, with outdoor seats under fragrant orange trees.

### ROTA DAS MARES

Rua da Junqueira 506. ☎ 213 642 857. Tues–Sun 10am–10pm. MAP P.88–89, POCKET MAP D4

Just far enough from the main sights to keep prices sensible, this spacious restaurant bustles at weekends with locals filling up with no-nonsense grills and fish; a full meal with wine should be under €14.

# Cafés

### ANTIGA CONFEITARIA DE BELÉM

Rua de Belém 90. Daily 8am–midnight. MAP P.88–89, POCKET MAP C4

No visit to Belém is complete without a coffee and hot *pastel de nata* (custard-cream tart) liberally sprinkled with *canela* (cinnamon) in this cavernous, tiled pastry shop and café, which has been serving them up since 1837. The place positively heaves, especially at weekends, but there's usually space to sit down in its warren of rooms.

### CAFÉ QUADRANTE

Centro Cultural de Belém. Mon–Fri 10am–8pm, Sat & Sun 10am–9pm. MAP P.88–89, POCKET MAP B4

Part of the Belém Cultural Centre, this café offers good-value self-service food from two counters. The best place to enjoy coffee and snacks is on the outdoor terrace by the roof gardens, overlooking the river. It's so popular with students that they are forbidden from studying here at mealtimes.

# Bars

### PIAZZA DI MARE

Avenida Brasília, Pavilhão Poente. Daily 11am–11pm. MAP P.88–89, POCKET MAP B9

Though you may baulk at paying €17 or more for the pasta and pizza dishes, this upmarket Italian restaurant also has an excellent riverside café-bar area where anyone can enjoy a modestly priced drink or cocktail facing the river.

ANTIGA CONFEITARIA DE BELÉM

# Avenida, Parque Eduardo VII and the Gulbenkian

Lisbon's main avenue, Avenida da Liberdade (simply known as "Avenida"), links the centre with its principal park, Parque Eduardo VII, best known for its views and enormous hothouses. The avenue, together with its side streets, was once home to statesmen and public figures. On its western side is the historic Praça das Amoreiras, the finishing point of the massive Águas Livres aqueduct. Here you'll find the Fundação Arpad Siznes-Viera da Silva, a collection of works by two artists heavily influenced by Lisbon. Northwest of the park, the Fundação Calouste Gulbenkian is undoubtedly Portugal's premier cultural centre, featuring one of Europe's richest art collections. Art-lovers have a further attraction to the east, where you can view the historic paintings and objects in the Casa Museu Dr Anastácio Gonçalves. Just north of here is the bullring at Campo Pequeno, while east lies the city's zoo.

## AVENIDA DA LIBERDADE

MAP P.96–97, POCKET MAP J5

The 1.3km, palm-lined Avenida da Liberdade is still much as poet Fernando Pessoa described it: "the finest artery in Lisbon… full of trees …small gardens, ponds, fountains, cascades and statues". It was laid out in 1882 as the city's main north-south avenue, and has several appealing outdoor cafés under the shade of trees that help cushion the

AVENIDA DA LIBERDADE

roar of the passing traffic. Some of the avenue's original nineteenth-century mansions remain, though most have been replaced by modern buildings. The upper end of the avenue houses many of the city's designer shops and airline offices and ends in a swirl of traffic at the landmark roundabout of Praça Marquês de Pombal, also known as Rotunda.

## PARQUE MAYER

MAP P.96–97, POCKET MAP J5

Opened in 1922 as an "entertainment precinct" when theatres were all the rage, the rundown Parque Mayer is still one of the capital's main destinations for theatregoers, though has long been earmarked for substantial renovation. This may lead to the controversial demolishing of the listed **Teatro Capitólio** – not the most handsome of theatres, but its concrete angular form is the country's first great Modernist structure.

## FUNDAÇÃO MEDEIROS E ALMEIDA

Rua Rosa Araújo 41 ☎ 213 547 892. �🌐 www. fundacaomedeirosealmeida.pt. Mon–Fri 1–5.30pm, Sat 10am–5.30pm. €5, free Sat 10am–1pm. MAP P.96–97, POCKET MAP H5

The Fundação Medeiros e Almeida was the home of the industrialist, philanthropist and art collector António Medeiros until his death in 1986. Today it serves as a showcase for his priceless series of artefacts. His collection of 225 Chinese porcelain items (some 2000 years old), sixteenth- to nineteenth-century watches, and English and Portuguese silverware are considered the most valuable in the world. Other highlights include glorious eighteenth-century azulejos in the Sala de Lago,

MURAL, PARQUE MAYER

a room complete with large water fountains; and a rare seventeenth-century clock, made for Queen Catherine of Bragança and mentioned by Samuel Pepys in his diary.

## PRAÇA DAS AMOREIRAS

MAP P.96–97, POCKET MAP G5

One of Lisbon's most tranquil squares, Praça das Amoreiras – complete with kids' play area – is dominated on its western side by the Águas Livres aqueduct (see p.98), with a chapel wedged into its arches.

On the south side the **Mãe d'Água** cistern (☎ 218 135 522; Mon–Sat 10am–6pm; €3) marks the end of the line for the aqueduct. Built between 1746 and 1834, the castellated stone building contains a reservoir that once supplied the city. The structure nowadays hosts occasional temporary art exhibitions. Head to the back where there are stairs leading on to the roof for great views over the city. Back on the square, the little kiosk café is a popular spot for a coffee or beer and also hosts occasional art exhibits.

Jardim
Zoológico

JARDIM
ZOOLÓGICO

Bus
Station

Sete Rios
Station

PRAÇA
DE
ESPANHA

PRAÇA DE
ESPANHA

CAMPOLIDE

Aqueduto das
Águas Livres

entrance to
Aqueduto

Amoreiras
Shopping
Center

AMOREIRAS

CAMPO DE
OURIQUE

**ACCOMMODATION**

| | |
|---|---|
| Eurostar das Letras | 10 |
| Fontana Park | 1 |
| Heritage Liberdade | 14 |
| Hotel Amazónia | 7 |
| Hotel Avenida Park | 4 |
| Hotel Britania | 8 |
| Hotel Dom Carlos Parque | 6 |
| Lisboa Plaza | 12 |
| NH Liberdade | 11 |
| Pousada de Juventude de Lisboa | 3 |
| Residencial Alegria | 13 |
| Sana Classic Rex | 5 |
| Sheraton Lisboa | 2 |
| Residencial Dom Sancho I | 9 |

**RESTAURANTS**

| | |
|---|---|
| O Cantinho de São José | 17 |
| Centro de Arte Moderno | 3 |
| Cervejaria Trindade | 1 |
| Eleven | 11 |
| Jardim do Sentidos | 18 |
| Marisqueira Santa Marta | 13 |
| Ribadouro | 16 |
| Rodízio Grill | 2 |
| Saldanha Mar | 8 |
| Solar do Morais | 7 |

**LIVE MUSIC**

| | |
|---|---|
| Hot Clube de Portugal | 1 |

**SHOPS**

| | |
|---|---|
| Amoreiras | 4 |
| Centro Colombo | 1 |
| El Corte Inglés | 2 |
| Mercado 31 de Janeiro | 3 |
| Mistura de Estilos | 5 |

**CAFÉS & BARS**

| | |
|---|---|
| A Linha d'Água | 10 |
| Bela Ipanema | 15 |
| Botequim do Rei | 12 |
| Boulevard Café | 6 |
| Galeto | 4 |
| Panorama Bar | 9 |
| Pastelaria Santa Marta | 14 |
| Versailles | 5 |

# Avenida, Parque Eduardo VII
# and the Gulbenkian

## FUNDAÇÃO ARPAD SIZNES-VIERA DA SILVA

Praça das Amoreiras 56–58 ☎ 213 880 044,
ⓦ www.fasvs.pt. Mon–Sun 10am–6pm. €3,
free Sun 10am–6pm. MAP P.96–97, POCKET MAP G5

The Fundação Arpad Siznes-Viera da Silva is a small but highly appealing gallery dedicated to the works of two painters and the artists who have been influenced by them. Arpad Siznes (1897–1985) was a Hungarian-born artist and friend of Henri Matisse and Pierre Bonnard, amongst others. While in Paris in 1928 he met the Portuguese artist Maria Helena Viera da Silva (1908–92), whose work was influenced by the surrealism of Joan Miró and Max Ernst, both of whom she was good friends with. Siznes and Viera da Silva married in 1930 and, in 1936, both exhibited in Lisbon, where they briefly lived, before eventually settling in France. The foundation shows the development of the artists' works, with Viera da Silva's more abstract, subdued paintings contrasting with flamboyant Siznes, some of whose paintings show the clear influence of Miró.

## AQUEDUTO DAS ÁGUAS LIVRES

Entrance on Calçada da Quintinha 6 ☎ 218
100 215. March–Oct daily 10am–6pm.
€3. Bus #718 from Amoreiras. MAP P.96–97,
POCKET MAP F4

The towering Aqueduto das Águas Livres (Free Waters Aqueduct) was opened in 1748, bringing a reliable source of safe drinking water to the city for the first time. Stretching for 60km (most of it underground), the aqueduct stood firm during the 1755 earthquake though it later gained a more notorious reputation thanks to one Diogo Alves, a nineteenth-century serial killer who threw his victims off the top – a seventy-metre drop. It is possible to walk across a 1.5km section of the aqueduct though you'll need a head for heights. The walkable section is accessed off a quiet residential street through a small park in Campolide, 1km north of Praça das Amoreiras.

## FUNDAÇÃO CALOUSTE GULBENKIAN

☎ 217 823 000, ⓦ www.gulbenkian.org. MAP
P.96–97, POCKET MAP H2

Set in extensive grounds, the Fundação Calouste Gulbenkian was set up by the Armenian oil magnate Calouste Gulbenkian (see box p.99) whose legendary art-market coups included the acquisition of works from the Hermitage in St Petersburg. Today the Gulbenkian Foundation has a multi-million dollar budget sufficient to finance work in all spheres of Portuguese cultural life. In this low-rise 1960s complex alone, it runs an orchestra, three concert halls and an attractive open-air amphitheatre.

AQUEDUTO DAS ÁGUAS LIVRES

## MUSEU CALOUSTE GULBENKIAN

Avenida de Berna ☎ 217 823 000, ⓦ www
.gulbenkian.pt. Tues–Sun 10am–5.45pm. €4,
free Sun, combined ticket with Centro de Arte
Moderna €7. MAP P.96–97, POCKET MAP H2

The Museu Calouste Gulbenkian covers virtually every
phase of Eastern and Western
art. The small Egyptian room
displays art from the Old
Kingdom (c.2700 BC) up to the
Roman period. Fine Roman
statues, silver and glass, and
gold jewellery from ancient
Greece follow. The Islamic arts
are magnificently represented
by a variety of ornamental
texts, opulently woven carpets,
glassware and Turkish tiles.
There is also porcelain from
China, and beautiful Japanese
prints and lacquer-work.

European art includes work
from all the major schools.
The seventeenth-century
collection yields Peter Paul
Rubens' graphic *The Love
of the Centaurs* (1635) and
Rembrandt's *Figure of an Old
Man*. Featured eighteenth-
century works include those
by Jean-Honoré Fragonard and
Thomas Gainsborough – in
particular the stunning *Portrait
of Mrs Lowndes-Stone*. The
big names of nineteenth- to

MUSEU CALOUSTE GULBENKIAN

twentieth-century France
– Manet, Monet, Degas,
Millet and Renoir – are all
represented, along with John
Sargent and Turner's vivid
*Wreck of a Transport Ship*
(1810). Elsewhere you'll find
Sèvres porcelain and furniture
from the reigns of Louis XV
and Louis XVI. The last room
features an amazing collection of Art Nouveau jewellery
by René Lalique. Don't miss
the fantastical *Peitoral-libélula*
(Dragonfly breastpiece)
brooch, decorated with enamel
work, gold and diamonds.

AVENIDA, PARQUE EDUARDO VII AND THE GULBENKIAN

## Calouste Gulbenkian

Calouste Sarkis Gulbenkian (1869–1955) was the Roman Abramovich
of his era, making his millions from oil but investing in the world's
best art rather than footballers. Born of wealthy Armenian parents in
Istanbul in 1869, he followed his father into the oil industry and eventually
moved to England. After the Russian Revolution of 1917 he bought works
from the Leningrad Hermitage. During World War II, his Turkish background
made him unwelcome in Britain and Gulbenkian auctioned himself to
whoever would have him. Portugal bid an aristocratic palace (a marquês was
asked to move out) and tax exemption, to acquire one of the most important
cultural patrons of the century. From 1942 to his death in 1955, he
accumulated one of the best private art collections in the world. His dying
wish was that all of his collection should be displayed in one place, and this
was granted in 1969 with the opening of the Museu Calouste Gulbenkian.

## CENTRO DE ARTE MODERNA JOSÉ AZEREDO PERDIGÃO

Main entrance on Rua Dr Nicolau de Bettencourt ☎ 217 823 000, ⓦ www .gulbenkian.org. Tues–Sun 10am–5.45pm. €4, free Sun, combined ticket with Museu Calouste Gulbenkian €7. MAP P.96–97, POCKET MAP H2

The Centro de Arte Moderna, part of the Gulbenkian foundation (see p.99), features pop art, installations and sculptures – some witty, some baffling, but all thought-provoking. Most of the big names on the twentieth-century Portuguese scene are included, including portraits and sketches by Almada Negreiros (1873–1970), the founder of *modernismo*, the bright Futurist colours of Amadeu de Sousa Cardoso, and works by Paula Rego, one of Portugal's leading contemporary artists, whose *Mãe* (1997) is outstanding. Pieces from major international artists such as David Hockney and Antony Gormley also feature, though these tend to be temporary.

PARQUE EDUARDO VII

## PARQUE EDUARDO VII

MAP P.96–97, POCKET MAP H4

The steep, formally laid-out Parque Eduardo VII was named to honour Britain's King Edward VII when he visited the city in 1903. Its main building is the ornately tiled Pavilhão dos Desportos (Sports Pavilion), which doubles as a concert venue. North of here is the main viewing platform which offers commanding vistas of the city as well as Ferris wheel during the summer months. Another highlight if you have children is the superb Parque Infantil (open daily; free), a play area built round a mock galleon.

Two huge, rambling **estufas** (daily: Estufa Fria April–Sept 9am–5.30pm; Oct–March 9am–4.30pm; Estufa Quente closes 30min earlier; €2) lie close by. Set in substantial former basalt quarries, both are filled with tropical plants, pools and endless varieties of palms and cacti. Of the two, the Estufa Quente (the hothouse) has the more exotic plants; the Estufa Fria (the coldhouse) hosts concerts and exhibitions.

Finally, the hilly northern reaches of the park contain an olive grove and a shallow lake which kids splash about in during the heat of the day.

## CASA MUSEU DR ANASTÁCIO GONÇALVES

Avda 5 de Outubro 6–8. Entrance on Rua Pinheiro Chagas ☎ 213 540 823, ⓦ www .cmag-ipmuseus.pt. Tues 2–6pm, Wed–Sun 10am–6pm. €3. MAP P.96–97, POCKET MAP J3

This appealing neo-Romantic building with Art Nouveau touches – including a beautiful stained-glass window – was originally built for painter José Malhoa in 1904, but now holds the exquisite private collection of ophthalmologist

Dr Anastácio Gonçalves, who bought the house in the 1930s. Highlights include paintings by Portuguese landscape artist João Vaz and by Malhoa himself, who specialized in historical paintings – his *Dream of Infante Henriques* is a typical example. You'll also find Chinese porcelain from the sixteenth-century Ming dynasty, along with furniture from England, France, Holland and Spain dating from the seventeenth century.

## PRAÇA DE TOUROS

Campo Pequeno ☎ 217 820 575 🖰 www .campopequeno.com. MAP P.96–97, POCKET MAP J1

Built in 1892, the Praça de Touros at Campo Pequeno is an impressive Moorish-style bullring seating nine thousand spectators. The Portuguese *tourada* (bullfight) is not as famous as its Spanish counterpart, but as a spectacle it's marginally preferable, as here the bull isn't killed in the ring, but instead is wrestled to the ground in a genuinely elegant, colourful and skilled display. During the fight, however, the bull is usually injured and slaughtered later in any case. Performances start at around

10pm on Thursday evenings from Easter to September. Surrounded by a ring of lively cafés and restaurants, the bullring also hosts visiting circuses and other events, while beneath is an underground shopping and cinema complex.

## JARDIM ZOOLÓGICO

Praça Marechal Humberto Delgado ☎ 217 232 900, 🖰 www.zoolisboa.pt. Daily: March– Sept 10am–8pm; Oct–Feb 10am–6pm. €16.50, children under 12 €12.50. MAP P.96–97, POCKET MAP E1

Lisbon's Jardim Zoológico was opened in 1884 and makes for an enjoyable excursion. There's a café-lined park area which you can visit for free and see monkeys, crocodiles and parrots. Once inside the zoo proper, a small cable car (daily from 11am until 30min before closing; included in the price) transports you over many of the animals, and there's a well-stocked reptile house (open 11am until 30min before closing) as further diversion. Just by its main gates lies the Animax amusement park (daily 11am–8pm), where kids can load up a card for rides and games to relieve their parents of further euros.

# Shops

## AMOREIRAS

Entrance on Avenida Engenheiro Duarte Pacheco. Daily 10am–midnight. Bus #758 or #58. MAP P.96–97, POCKET MAP F4

Amoreiras, Lisbon's striking, postmodern commercial centre, is a wild fantasy of pink and blue towers sheltering ten cinemas, sixty cafés and restaurants, 250 shops and a hotel. Built in 1985 and designed by adventurous Portuguese architect Tomás Taveira, most of its stores are open daily; Sunday sees the heaviest human traffic, with entire families descending for an afternoon out.

## CENTRO COLOMBO

Avenida Lusíada. Most shops daily 10am–midnight. Metro Colégio Militar/Luz. MAP P.96–97, POCKET MAP F1

Iberia's largest shopping centre is almost a town in its own right, with over 400 shops, 65 restaurants and 11 cinema screens. Major stores include FNAC, C&A, Zara, Habitat and Toys "R" Us, while the top floor has the usual fast-food outlets along with a sit-down dining area in the jungle-themed "Cidade Perdida" (Lost City). There is also a "Fun Centre" (daily: noon–midnight) which claims to be Europe's largest covered amusement park, complete with rides, bumper cars, ten-pin bowling and even a roller coaster that whizzes overhead. An additional outdoor area features mini-bungee jumps, a go-kart track and toy car and boat rides.

## EL CORTE INGLÊS

Avda António Augusto de Aguiar. Most shops Mon–Sat 10am–10pm. Cinema info on ☎ 707 232 221. MAP P.96–97, POCKET MAP H3

A giant Spanish department store spread over nine floors, two of which are underground. The basement specializes in gourmet food, with various delis, bakers and a supermarket (closed Sun afternoon), while the upper floors offer a range of stylish goods, including clothes, sports gear, books, CDs and toys. The top floor packs in cafés and restaurants with an outdoor terrace. There's also a fourteen-screen cinema in the basement.

## MERCADO 31 DE JANEIRO

Rua Enginheiro Viera da Silva. Daily 9am–6pm. MAP P.96–97, POCKET MAP J3

This bustling local market is divided into sections; you'll find a colourful array of fresh fruit, vegetables, spices, fish, flowers and a few crafts.

## MISTURA DE ESTILOS

Rua São José 21. Mon–Fri 3–8pm. MAP P.96–97, POCKET MAP J5

This tiny shop sells individually crafted tiles from around €3 – as the name implies, the styles are mixed – from plain patterns to lovely animal motifs – but most are simple, effective and portable.

EL CORTE INGLÊS

# Restaurants

### O CANTINHO DE SÃO JOSÉ

Rua São José 94 ☎ 213 427 866. Mon–Fri &
Sun noon–10pm. MAP P.96–97, POCKET MAP J5

Friendly *tasca* serving generous
portions at bargain prices –
tuck into a full meal of grilled
meat, salmon or other fish with
wine and you may get change
from €10.

### CENTRO DE ARTE MODERNA

Rua Dr Bettencourt, Fundação Calouste
Gulbenkian. Tues–Sun 10am–5.45pm. MAP
P.96–97, POCKET MAP H2

Join the lunchtime queues at
the museum restaurant for
bargain hot and cold dishes.
There's an excellent choice of
salads for vegetarians. Similar
food is offered in the basement
of the Gulbenkian museum,
with outdoor seats facing the
gardens.

### CERVEJARIA TRINDADE

Centro de Lazer de Campo Pequeno 601
☎ 217 964 000. Daily 10am–midnight. MAP
P.96–97, POCKET MAP JI

This branch of the historic
beerhall (see p.67) is set within
the outer ring of the bullring,
with outdoor seats on the
square. There's a relatively short
list, but the *bacalhau* dishes
and steaks are recom-mended.
Mains from €9.

### ELEVEN

Rua Marquês da Fronteira ☎ 213 862 211,
ⓦ www.restauranteeleven.com. Mon–Sat
12.30–3pm & 7.30–11pm. MAP P.96–97, POCKET
MAP G4

At the top of Parque Eduardo
VII, this Michelin-starred
restaurant hits the heights both
literally and metaphorically.
The interior is both intimate
and bright with wonderful city
views. The food is expensive
but not outrageous, with set
menus from around €75 or a

ELEVEN

tasting menu at around €90.
Dishes feature Azorean tuna
with sesame, veal with lemon
grass or scallops in pistachio
crust, and there's a fine wine
list.

### JARDIM DO SENTIDOS

Rua Mãe d'Água 3 ☎ 213 423 670. Mon–Fri
noon–3pm & 7–10.30pm, Sat 7–10.30pm. MAP
P.96–97, POCKET MAP J5

This attractive, long space
opens onto a lovely garden. The
food is vegetarian, with good-
value dishes such as a sublime
*tofu á bras* and decent lasagne
from around €9.

### MARISQUEIRA SANTA MARTA

Trav. do Enviado de Inglaterra 1 (off Rua de
Santa Marta) ☎ 213 525 638. Daily 9am–
midnight. MAP P.96–97, POCKET MAP J4

Attractive and spacious
*marisqueira* with bubbling
tanks of crabs in one corner.
Service is very attentive and
meals end with a complimen-
tary port, after which you don't
usually care that the bill is
slightly above average (mains
from €10).

### RIBADOURO

Avda da Liberdade 155 ☎ 213 549 411. Daily noon–1am. MAP P.96–97, POCKET MAP J5

The *avenida*'s best *cervejaria*, serving superb mixed grills (around €13), speciality prawns with garlic (around €15) and pricier shellfish (but no fish). If you don't fancy a full meal, take a seat at the bar and order a beer with a plate of prawns. It's best to book for the restaurant, especially at weekends.

### RODÍZIO GRILL

Campo Pequeno 79 ☎ 217 939 760. Mon–Sat noon–4pm & 8pm–midnight. MAP P.96–97, POCKET MAP J1

Right opposite the bullring, this huge, industrial place appropriately specializes in Brazilian *rodízio* – various types of barbecued meats – with a salad bar as a token healthy option. It's good value if you have a big appetite as, for around €25, you can top your plate up as often as you like.

### SALDANHA MAR

Rua Eng. Viera da Silva 2E ☎ 210 410 620. Daily 12.30–3pm & 7.30–11pm. MAP P.96–97, POCKET MAP J3

Chic, minimalist restaurant attached to the cool *Fontana Park* hotel (see p.134). Most of the sumptuous fish and seafood is shipped straight from the market opposite, combined with fresh seasonal produce; dishes such as sea bass with sautéed vegetables and filling fish stews start at around €14.

### SOLAR DO MORAIS

Rua Augusto dos Santos 3. Mon–Fri 9.30am–10.30pm. MAP P.96–97, POCKET MAP H3

A popular lunchtime spot for locals, despite its position between the tourist draws of Parque Eduardo VII and the Gulbenkian. The cool, arched interior has cabinets of fresh

A LINHA D'ÁGUA

food, bottles lining the walls and a large ham on the bar. Good-value trout and salmon dishes are always worth ordering, and there's a small outdoor terrace.

# Cafés and bars

### A LINHA D'ÁGUA

Parque Eduardo VII. Daily 10am–8pm. MAP P.96–97, POCKET MAP G3

Facing a small lake, this glass-fronted café is at the northern end of the park. It's a tranquil spot to sip a coffee or beer, and decent buffet lunches are served too.

### BELA IPANEMA

Avda da Liberdade 169. Mon–Sat 7am–midnight. MAP P.96–97, POCKET MAP J5

A bustling café/bar/restaurant by the São Jorge cinema where a steady stream of locals pops in for pastries, light lunches, beers and coffees at the bar, or in its small dining area that serves very good-value food; outdoor tables face the avenue.

## BOTEQUIM DO REI

Esplanade da Parque Eduardo VII. Tues–Sun 10am–9pm. MAP P.96–97, POCKET MAP H3

The fish and meat dishes on offer here are fairly average but the outdoor seating, right in the park by a small lake, is particularly tranquil, making this a good place to head for lunch or a drink. Take care here, though, after dark.

## BOULEVARD CAFÉ

Avda Praia da Vitória 35a. Mon–Sat 7am–2am. MAP P.96–97, POCKET MAP J3

One of the few lively café-bars in these parts, a bright, modern space attracting a young crowd for coffees and cakes by day and drinks or decent-value meals in the evening, when the music drowns out the TV sets in the corners.

## GALETO

Avda da República 14 ☎ 213 560 269. Daily 7am–4am. MAP P.96–97, POCKET MAP J2

Late-opening café/bar/restaurant with striking 1950s decor: dark, metal-studded walls and padded bar seats. There's a great range of snacks, pastries, beers and coffees, or you can perch at the bar for a full meal at sensible prices.

## PANORAMA BAR

Sheraton Lisboa, Rua Latino Coelho 1. Daily noon–midnight. MAP P.96–97, POCKET MAP J3

Stroll into this high-rise hotel and take the lift to the spectacular top-floor bar (open to the public). As you'd expect, drinks aren't cheap, but dubbed Lisbon's eighth hill, the bar commands the best views of the city you'll find outside of a plane.

## PASTELARIA SANTA MARTA

Rua Rodrigues Sampaio 52. Mon–Sat 7am–9pm. MAP P.96–97, POCKET MAP J5

Unglamorous but popular local haunt with a superb array of cakes and snacks. A good spot for inexpensive lunches. Pay at the till on exit.

## VERSAILLES

Avda da República 15a. Daily 7.30am–10pm. MAP P.96–97, POCKET MAP J2

Traditional café full of bustling waiters circling the starched tablecloths. It's busiest at around 4pm, when Lisbon's elderly dames gather for a chat beneath the chandeliers.

# Live music

## HOT CLUBE DE PORTUGAL

Praça da Alegria 39 ☎ 213 467 369. ⓦ www .hcp.pt. Tues–Sat 10pm–2am. MAP P.96–97, POCKET MAP J5

Dating from 1948 – making it one of Europe's oldest jazz clubs – this tiny basement club hosts top names in the jazz world, along with a range of local performers. Check the website as the venue may relocate to a nearby premises after a recent fire.

VERSAILLES

# Parque das Nações

The Parque das Nações or "Park of Nations" (pronounced "na-soysh") is the high-tech former site of Expo 98. Its flat, pedestrianized walkways lined with fountains and futuristic buildings are in complete contrast to the narrow, precipitous streets of old Lisbon, and it is packed with locals on summer weekends. The main highlight is the giant Oceanário de Lisboa, but it also features a casino, a cable car, riverside walk- and cycle-ways, a giant park and two of Lisbon's largest concert venues. It is also impossible to miss the astonishing 17km-long Vasco da Gama bridge over the Tejo. Constructed in time for the Expo in 1998, it is still the longest bridge in Europe.

## OLIVAIS DOCK AND THE PAVILHÃO ATLÂNTICO

MAP P.107, POCKET MAP B17–18

The central focus of the Parque das Nações is the Olivais dock, overlooked by pixie-hatted twin towers, and where boats pull in on Tejo cruises (see p.142). The dock's **Nautical Centre** (☎218 918 532) offers canoeing, sailing and windsurfing lessons. The main building facing the dock is the Pavilhão de Portugal (Portugal Pavilion), a multipurpose arena designed by Álvaro Siza Vieira,

architect of the reconstructed Chiado district, featuring an enormous, sagging concrete canopy on its south side. Opposite here – past Antony Gormley's weird Rhizone sculpture, a tree of cast-iron legs – is the spaceship-like **Pavilhão Atlântico** (Atlantic Pavilion; ☎218 918 440, ⓦwww.pavilhaoatlantico .pt), Portugal's largest indoor arena and the venue for major visiting bands and sporting events. The MTV music awards were held here in 2005.

## Visiting the park

The best way to reach the park is to take the metro to Oriente or bus #28 from Praça do Comércio. Oriente metro station exits in the bowels of the Estação do Oriente, a cavernous glass and concrete station designed by Spanish architect Santiago Calatrava.

The park's Posto de Informação (information desk; daily 10am–8pm, until 7pm from Oct–April; ☎218 919 333, ⓦwww.portaldasnacoes.pt) has details of the day's events. If you want to visit everything, it is worth buying a Cartão do Parque (€17.50, or €9 for children under 12) from the desk. This allows free access to the main sights and discounts at other attractions.

It's easy to walk round the park, or there's a toy train, which trundles anticlockwise around the main sights (hourly 10am–7pm; until 5pm from Oct–April; €2.50). You can also hire bikes from Tejo Bike (ⓦwww.tejobike .pt) behind the information desk for €5 an hour.

# Parque das Nações

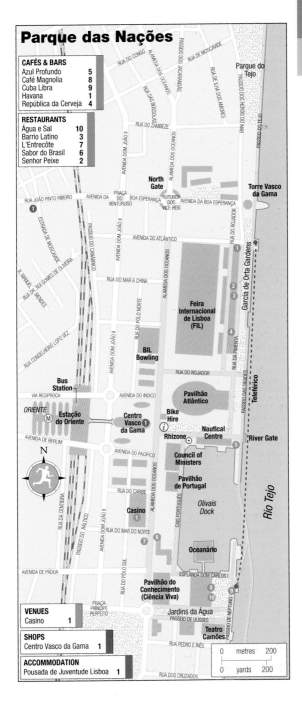

**CAFÉS & BARS**
| | |
|---|---|
| Azul Profundo | 5 |
| Café Magnolia | 8 |
| Cuba Libra | 9 |
| Havana | 1 |
| República da Cerveja | 4 |

**RESTAURANTS**
| | |
|---|---|
| Água e Sal | 10 |
| Barrio Latino | 3 |
| L'Entrecôte | 7 |
| Sabor do Brasil | 6 |
| Senhor Peixe | 2 |

**VENUES**
| | |
|---|---|
| Casino | 1 |

**SHOPS**
| | |
|---|---|
| Centro Vasco da Gama | 1 |

**ACCOMMODATION**
| | |
|---|---|
| Pousada de Juventude Lisboa | 1 |

## PAVILHÃO DO CONHECIMENTO (CIÊNCIA VIVA)

Alameda dos Oceanos ☎ 218 917 100,
ⓦ www.pavconhecimento.pt. Tues–Fri
10am–6pm, Sat & Sun 11am–7pm. €7,
children under 17 €4. MAP P.107, POCKET MAP B18

Run by Portugal's Ministry
of Science and Technology,
the Knowledge Pavilion
(Live Science) hosts excellent changing exhibitions on
subjects like 3D animation and
the latest computer technology,
and is usually bustling with
school parties. The permanent
interactive exhibits – allowing
you to create a vortex in water
or a film of detergent the size of
a baby's blanket – are particularly good and there's also a
cybercafé offering free internet.

## JARDINS DA ÁGUA

MAP P.107, POCKET MAP B19

The Jardins da Água (Water
Gardens), crisscrossed by
waterways and ponds, are
based on the stages of a river's
drainage pattern, from stream
to estuary. They are not huge,
but linked by stepping stones,
and there are enough gushing
fountains, water gadgets

and pumps to keep children
occupied for hours.

## OCEANÁRIO

☎ 218 917 002, ⓦ www.oceanario.pt. Daily
May–Sept 10am–8pm, Oct–April 10am–7pm.
€12, children under 12 €6, family ticket €29.
MAP P.107, POCKET MAP B18

Designed by Peter Chermaeff
and looking like something
off the set of a James Bond
film, the Oceanário de Lisboa
(Lisbon Oceanarium), one of
Europe's largest, contains some
8,000 fish and marine animals
representing 450 species. Its
main feature is the enormous
central tank which you can
look into from different levels
for close-up views of circling
sharks down to the rays
burying themselves into the
sand. Almost more impressive,
though, are the re-creations
of various ocean ecosystems,
such as the Antarctic tank,
containing frolicking penguins,
and the Pacific tank, where
otters bob about in the rock
pools. On a darkened lower
level, smaller tanks contain
shoals of brightly coloured
tropical fish and other warm-
water creatures. Find a window
free of school parties and the
whole experience becomes the
closest you'll get to deep-sea
diving without getting wet.

## THE TELEFÉRICO AND THE JARDINS GARCIA DA ORTA

Mid-June to mid-Sept Mon–Fri 11am–8pm,
Sat & Sun 10am–8pm; Mid-Sept to mid-June
daily 10am–7pm. €4 one-way, €6 return.
Children under 14 €2 single, €3.30 return. MAP
P.107, POCKET MAP B16–18

The ski-lift-style *teleférico*
(cable car) rises up to 20m as it
shuttles you over Olivais Docks
to the northern side of the
Parque, giving commanding
views over the site on the way.
It drops down to the Garcia da
Orta gardens, containing exotic

FOUNTAIN IN CAMINHO DA ÁGUA

VASCO DA GAMA BRIDGE

trees from Portugal's former colonies. Behind the gardens, Rua Pimenta is lined with a motley collection of international restaurants, from Irish to Israeli.

### TORRE VASCO DA GAMA

MAP P.107, POCKET MAP B16

Once an integral part of an oil refinery, the Torre Vasco da Gama (Vasco da Gama Tower) is, at 145m high, Lisbon's tallest structure. The tower is currently being converted into a five-star hotel.

### PARQUE DO TEJO

MAP P.107, POCKET MAP B15

Spreading along the waterfront for 2km right up to the Vasco da Gama bridge, Parque do Tejo is Lisbon's newest park, with bike trails and riverside walks. It's a great spot for a picnic – supplies are available from the supermarkets in the Vasco da Gama shopping centre and bike hire from Tejo Bike (see p.106).

### FEIRA INTERNACIONAL DE LISBOA

☎ 218 921 500, ✪ www.fil.pt. MAP P.107, POCKET MAP B16–17

Lisbon's trade fair hall, the Feira Internacional de Lisboa (FIL), hosts various events, including a handicrafts fair displaying ceramics and crafts from around the country (usually in July).

## Vasco da Gama

The opening of Parque das Nações in 1998 celebrated the 500th anniversary of Vasco da Gama's arrival in India. One of Portugal's greatest explorers, Da Gama was born in Sines in 1460. By the 1490s he was working for João II protecting trading stations along the African coast. This persuaded the next king, Manuel I, to commission him to find a sea route to India. He departed Lisbon in July 1497 with a fleet of four ships, reaching southern Africa in December. The following May they finally reached Calicut in southwest India, obtaining trading terms before departing in August, 1498. The return voyage took a full year, by which time Da Gama had lost two of his ships and half his men. But he was richly rewarded by the king, his voyage inspiring Camões to write *Os Lusiadas*, Portugal's most famous epic poem. Da Gama returned to India twice more, the final time in 1524 when he contracted malaria and died in the town of Cochin.

CENTRO VASCO DA GAMA

less has well prepared and moderately priced dishes such as game sausages, pumpkin risottos and pasta from around €10. The best tables are on the outdoor terrace facing a sculpted lawn and the cable car.

### BARRIO LATINO

Rua de Pimenta 31 ☏ 913 497 1585, ⓦ www .barriolatinolisboa.com. Daily noon–3am. MAP P.107, POCKET MAP B16.

A decent bar and restaurant (steak and fish from around €12) but best known for its riotous Afro-Latin dance nights; from Wed to Sun there are dance lessons, or just come along and join in the fun.

### L'ENTRECÔTE

Alameda dos Oceanos 10212a ☏ 218 962 220. Daily 12.30–3pm & 7.30–11pm. MAP P.107, POCKET MAP B18

Local branch of the Lisbon restaurant famed for its fabulous steaks cooked with sublime sauces – choose from two menus starting at €15.

### SABOR DO BRASIL

Alameda dos Oceanos 1990 ☏ 218 955 143. Daily noon–3am & 7.30–11pm. MAP P.107, POCKET MAP B18

This large space has outdoor seats in a great position facing the waters. Its name means "taste of Brazil" and you can sample a range of piquant dishes such as spicy *moqueca* fish, tropical salmon, *feijoada* bean stews or *picanha* garlic beef from €9–14.

### SENHOR PEIXE

Rua da Pimenta ☏ 218 955 892. Tues–Sat noon–3am & 7.30–11pm, Sun noon–3pm. MAP P.107, POCKET MAP B16

"Mr Fish" is widely thought to serve up some of the best fresh seafood in the Lisbon region – check the counter for the day's catch or choose a lobster from the bubbling tank. Most dishes

# Shops

### CENTRO VASCO DA GAMA

Avda D. João II ☏ 218 930 601, ⓦ www .centrovascodagama.pt. MAP P.107, POCKET MAP A17

Three floors of local and international stores are housed under a glass roof, washed by permanently running water; international branches include Zara, Timberland, Massimo Dutti and C&A and local sports and bookshops also feature. There are plenty of fast-food outlets and good-value restaurants on the top floor, ten cinema screens, children's areas and a huge Continente supermarket on the lower floor.

# Restaurants

### ÁGUA E SAL

Esplanada Dom Carols I 31 ☏ 218 936 189. Daily noon–4pm & 8pm–midnight. MAP P.107, POCKET MAP B18

In a bit of a glass box behind the Oceanarium, this neverthe-

– from around €15 – are grilled in the open kitchen. There's also a little fish-themed bar and pleasant outdoor tables facing the river.

# Cafés and bars

### AZUL PROFUNDO

Doca da Olivais. Daily 10am–2am, closes 7pm from Oct–April. MAP P.107, POCKET MAP B17

Sunny esplanade bar overlooking the glittering docks. Offers a good range of snacks, fruit juices and fantastic *caipirinha* cocktails along with inexpensive lunches.

### CAFÉ MAGNOLIA

Esplanada Dom Carols 29 ☎ 218 968 214. Daily 10am–8pm (closes 7pm from Oct–April). MAP P.107, POCKET MAP B18

Adjoined to but independent of the Oceanarium, this bright little café has a counter stuffed with excellent pastries. It also does inexpensive toasts and filled crepes, with outdoor seating facing a pleasant lawned area and the river.

COFFEE AND PASTEL DE NATA

### CUBA LIBRA

Passeio de Neptuno. Daily noon–4am, closes 7pm from Oct–April. MAP P.107, POCKET MAP B18

Breezy kiosk café-bar right by the river and under the cable-car run. It comes into its own on a warm evening when the *caipirinha* cocktails and rum punches lubricate proceedings. Also does decent toasts and burgers.

### HAVANA

Rua da Pimenta 115–117. Daily noon–4am, closed Tues Oct–April. MAP P.107, POCKET MAP B16

Lively Cuban bar with an airy interior and outdoor seating. The pulsating Latin sounds get progressively louder after 11pm, when it turns into more of a club until 4am.

### REPÚBLICA DA CERVEJA

Passeio das Tágides 2–26 ☎ 218 922 590. Daily 12.30pm–1am. MAP P.107, POCKET MAP B17

In a great position close to the water's edge and facing the Vasco da Gama bridge, this modern bar-restaurant specializes in some fine international beers, though sticking to the local Superbock will save a few euros. Steaks, burgers and German cuisine are also on offer (mains from €8), and there's live music Thurs–Sat.

# Live music

### CASINO

Alameda dos Oceanos ☎ 218 929 000, ⓦ www.casinolisboa.pt. Sun–Thurs 3pm–3am, Fri–Sat 4pm–4am. MAP P.107, POCKET MAP A18

Opened in 2006, this state-of-the-art space – with its glass cylinder entrance hall – hosts top shows from Broadway and London as well as major concerts in the performance hall, which has a retractable roof. The usual casino attractions also feature.

# Sintra

If you make just one day-trip from Lisbon, choose the beautiful hilltop town of Sintra, the former summer residence of Portuguese royalty and a UNESCO World Heritage Site since 1995. Not only does the town boast two of Portugal's most extraordinary palaces, it also contains a semitropical garden, a Moorish castle, a top modern-art museum and proximity to some great beaches. Looping around a series of wooded ravines and with a climate that encourages moss and ferns to grow from every nook and cranny, Sintra consists of three districts: Sintra-Vila, with most of the historical attractions; Estefânia, a ten-minute walk to the east, where trains from Lisbon pull in; and São Pedro to the south, well known for its antique shops and best visited on the eve of São Pedro (June 28–29), the main saint's day, and for its market on the second and fourth Sunday of the month.

## SINTRA MUSEU DE ARTE MODERNA

Avenida Heliodoro Salgado ☎ 219 248 170, Ⓦ www.berardocollection.com. Tues–Sun 10am–6pm, free. MAP OPPOSITE

A short walk from Sintra's station, the Museu de Arte Moderna houses a small part of one of Iberia's best collections of modern art, amassed by Madeiran tobacco magnate Joe Berardo. The bulk of his art can be seen in Lisbon's Berardo Collection (see p.89), but you can still see some top artists here in Sintra's former casino. The collection spreads over three floors, but there is only space to show twenty works at any one time, alongside temporary exhibits. Depending on when you visit, you might see works by Jackson Pollock, David Hockney, Roy Lichtenstein and Andy Warhol.

## Visiting Sintra

Sintra is served by regular trains from Lisbon's Rossio, Entre Campos and Sete Rios station (every 15–20min; 45min; €1.70 single). A land train (every 30min from 10.30am–dusk; €5 day ticket) runs from Sintra station to São Pedro and back via Sintra-Vila. Alternatively, bus #434 takes a circular route from Sintra station or Sintra-Vila to most of the sites mentioned in this chapter (every 15min; €4.50) and allows you to get on and off whenever you like on the circuit. You can also hire electric bikes from opposite the tourist office (daily 10am–6pm, €30 a day; Ⓦ www.mup .pt). To see the area around Sintra, including the coast, consider a Day-rover (Turístico Diário) ticket on the local Scotturb buses (Ⓦ www.scotturb.com; €10). Ask at the tourist office about various combined tickets that can save money on entry to the main sites.

## Sintra

- Centro Cultural O. Cadaval
- Market **1**
- Museu de Arte Moderna **2**
- Câmara Municipal **1** **2**
- Train Station ⓘ
- ESTEFÂNIA
- see Sintra-Vila
- SINTRA-VILA
- Quinta da Regaleira ⓘ
- Parque da Liberdade
- Castelo dos Mouros
- Santa Maria
- SÃO PEDRO DE SINTRA
- São Pedro **3**
- Ticket Office
- SANTA EUFÉMIA
- P
- Palácio da Pena **P**
- Ticket Office

Street labels: AV. ADRIANO COELHO, RUA A. BOCAGE, RUA VEIGA DA CUNHA, RUA CÂMARA PESTANA, JUNIOR, AV. DR. ÁLVARO DE VASCONCELOS, AV. MOVIMENTO DAS FORÇAS ARMADAS, AL. DOS COM. DA GUERRA, ESTRADA DA MACIEIRA, RUA SOTTO MAYOR, R. DA MADEIRA, R. GUILHERME, LARGO DR. VIRGÍLIO HORTA, R. ALFREDO DA COSTA, LARGO D. MANUEL I, RUA GAGO COUTINHO, R. JOÃO DE DEUS, R. DR. ANDRÉ DE ALBUQUERQUE, RUA AUGUSTO FREIRE, LARGO FERNANDO MORAIS, RUA DAS MURTAS, RUA CONDE SEXAL, CAMINHO DA ALBA LONGA, RUA J. DOS SANTOS, VOLTA DO DUQUE, RUA EUGÉNIO C. PEDROSA, F. NAVARRO, RUA VISCONDE DE MONSERRATE, RUA MARECHAL SALDANHA, CALÇ. DOS CLÉRIGOS, RIBEIRO, CALÇADA DE S. PEDRO, CALÇADA DA PENALVA, RUA SERPA PINTO, ESTRADA DA PENA, RUA M

Scale: 0 metres 100 / 0 yards 100

## Sintra-Vila

Street labels: RUA SOTTO MAYOR, RUA PASSEIO DOS VELHOS, RUA CONS. SEGURADO, LARGO RAINHA D. AMÉLIA, CALÇADA DO RIO DO PORTO, CALÇADA DO, RUA DA PENDOA, RUA FRESCA, PRAÇA DA REPÚBLICA, VOLTA DO DUQUE, RUA GIL VICENTE, RUA CONSELHEIRO V. PEDROSO, RUA FONTE DA PIPA, RUA DA FERRARIA, LARGO FERREIRA DE CASTRO, RUA A. EUGENIA F. NAVARRO, RUA VISCONDE DE MONSERRATE

- Palácio Nacional
- Museu do Brinquedo

| ACCOMMODATION | |
|---|---|
| Chalet Relogio | 4 |
| Pensão Nova Sintra | 2 |
| Piela's | 1 |
| Residencial Sintra | 3 |

| RESTAURANTS | |
|---|---|
| Alcobaça | 7 |
| Cantinho de São Pedro | 3 |
| Páteo do Garrett | 10 |
| A Tasca do Manel | 1 |
| Tulhas | 8 |

| CAFÉS | |
|---|---|
| Adega das Caves | 5 |
| Café Paris | 4 |
| Casa Piriquita | 6 |
| Fábrica das Verdadeiras Queijadas da Sapa | 2 |

| BARS & CLUBS | |
|---|---|
| Bar Fonte da Pipa | 9 |

PALACIO NACIONAL

## PALÁCIO NACIONAL

Largo da Rainha Dona Amélia 🕿 219 106
840 🌐 www.imc.pt. Mon, Tues & Thurs–Sun
9.30am–5.30pm. €7, free Sun 10am–2pm.
MAP P.113

Best seen early or late in the
day to avoid the crowds, the
sumptuous Palácio Nacional
was probably already in
existence at the time of the
Moors. It takes its present form
from the rebuilding of Dom
João I (1385–1433) and his
successor, Dom Manuel I, the
chief royal beneficiary of Vasco
da Gama's explorations. Its
exterior style is an amalgam of
Gothic – featuring impressive
battlements – and Manueline,
tempered inside by a good deal
of Moorish influences. Sadly,
after the fall of the monarchy in
1910, most of the surrounding
walls and medieval houses
were destroyed. Highlights
on the lower floor include the
Manueline **Sala dos Cisnes**,
so-called for the swans (*cisnes*)
on its ceiling, and the Sala das
Pegas, which takes its name
from the flock of magpies
(*pegas*) painted on the frieze
and ceiling – João I, caught in
the act of kissing a lady-in-
waiting by his queen, reputedly

had the room decorated with
as many magpies as there were
women at court, to imply they
were all magpie-like gossips.

Best of the upper floor is the
gallery above the palace chapel.
Beyond, a succession of **state
rooms** finishes with the Sala
das Brasões, its domed and
coffered ceiling emblazoned
with the arms of 72 noble
families. Finally, don't miss the
kitchens, whose roofs taper
into the giant chimneys that
are the palace's distinguishing
features. The Palace also hosts
events for the Sintra Music
Festival (see p.146).

## MUSEU DO BRINQUEDO

Rua Visconde de Monserrate 29 🕿 219
242 171, 🌐 www.museu-do-brinquedo.pt.
Tues–Sun 10am–6pm. €4, children under 12
€2. MAP P.113

Housed in a former fire station,
the Museu do Brinquedo
– a fascinating private toy
collection – is a great place
for children. The huge array
of toys exhibited over three
floors is somewhat confusingly
labelled, but look out for the
3000-year-old stone Egyptian
toys on the first floor, the 1930s
Hornby trains and some of the

first-ever toy cars, produced in Germany in the early 1900s. There are numerous cases of soldiers, early Portuguese toys including a selection of 1930s beach games, wooden toys from Senegal, wire bicycles from Zimbabwe, and a top floor stuffed with dolls and doll's house furniture. There's also a café and a small play area for young children.

## QUINTA DA REGALEIRA

Daily: Feb–March & Oct 10am–6.30pm; April–Sept 10am–8pm; Nov–Jan 10am–5.30pm. Tours (90min) every 30min–60min; advance booking essential on ☎ 219 106 650; €10. Unguided visits €6. MAP P.113

The Quinta da Regaleira is one of Sintra's most elaborate estates. It was designed at the end of the nineteenth century by Italian architect and theatre set designer Luigi Manini for wealthy Brazilian merchant António Augusto Carvalho Monteiro. Manini's penchant for the dramatic is obvious: the principal building, the mock-Manueline Palácio dos Milhões, sprouts turrets and towers while the interior boasts Art Nouveau tiles and elaborate Rococo wooden ceilings.

The surrounding **gardens** shelter fountains, terraces and grottoes, with the highlight being the Initiation Well, inspired by the initiation practices of the Freemasons. Entering via a Harry Potter-esque revolving stone door, you walk down a moss-covered spiral staircase to the foot of the well and through a tunnel, which eventually resurfaces at the edge of a lake (though in winter you exit from a shorter tunnel so as not to disturb a colony of hibernating bats).

In summer, the gardens host occasional performances of live music, usually classical or jazz.

## CASTELO DOS MOUROS

☎ 219 237 300, ⓦ www.parquedesintra .pt. Daily: April–mid Sept 9.30am–8pm; mid-Sept–March 10am–6pm. €6. MAP P.113

Reached on bus #434, or a steep drive, the ruined ramparts of the Castelo dos Mouros are truly spectacular. Built in the ninth century, the Moorish castle spans two rocky pinnacles, with the remains of a mosque spread midway between, and extraordinary views all around. Conquered in 1147 by Afonso Henriques, with the aid of Scandinavian Crusaders, the castle walls fell into disrepair over subsequent centuries, before Ferdinand II had them restored in the mid-nineteenth century.

If walking from Sintra, take Calçada dos Clérigos, near the church of Santa Maria. From here, a stone pathway leads all the way up to the lower slopes, where you can see a Moorish grain silo and a ruined twelfth-century church. To enter the castle itself, you'll need to walk further along the path to buy a ticket from the road exit and double back to the castle.

CASTELO DOS MOUROS

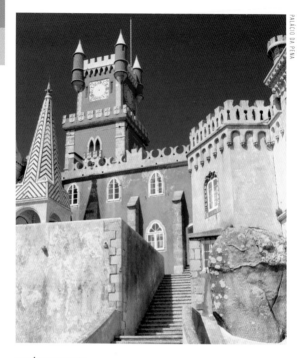

## PALÁCIO DA PENA

Estrada da Pena ☎ 219 237 300, ✆ www
.parquedesintra.pt. Daily: April–Sept
9.45am–7pm; Oct–March 10am–6pm; last
entry 1hr before closing. Palace and gardens
€12 (€8 from Oct to March), gardens only
€6. MAP P.113

Bus #434 stops opposite the
lower entrance to Parque da
Pena, a stretch of rambling
woodland with a scattering
of lakes and follies. At the
top of the park, about twenty
minutes' walk from the
entrance or a short ride on a
shuttle bus (€2 return), looms
the fabulous **Palácio da Pena**, a
wild fantasy of domes, towers,
ramparts and walkways,
approached through mock-
Manueline gateways and a
drawbridge that does not draw.
A compelling riot of kitsch, the
palace was built in the 1840s to
the specifications of Ferdinand of Saxe-Coburg-Gotha,
husband of Queen Maria II,
with the help of the German
architect, Baron Eschwege. The
interior is preserved exactly as
it was left by the royal family
when they fled Portugal in
1910. The result is fascinating:
rooms of stone decorated to
look like wood, statues of
turbaned Moors nonchalantly
holding electric chandeliers
– it's all here. Of an original
convent, founded in the early
sixteenth century to celebrate
the first sight of Vasco da
Gama's returning fleet, only
a beautiful, tiled chapel and
Manueline cloister have been
retained.

Above Pena, a marked
footpath climbs in thirty
minutes or so to the **Cruz Alta**,
the highest point of the Serra
de Sintra, at 529m.

## MONSERRATE

Estrada da Monserrate ☎ 219 237 300.
Daily: April–Sept 9.30am–8pm; Oct–March
10am–6pm. €5. Guided tours to palace daily
at 10am & 3pm, €5 extra. MAP BELOW

The name most associated
with the fabulous gardens and
palace of Monserrate is that of
William Beckford, the wealthiest untitled Englishman of
his age, who rented the estate
from 1793 to 1799, having been
forced to flee Britain after he
was caught in a compromising
position with a sixteen-year-old
boy. Setting about improving
the place, he landscaped a
waterfall and even imported a
flock of sheep from his estate.

Half a century later, a second
immensely rich Englishman,
Sir Francis Cook, bought the
estate and imported the head
gardener from Kew to lay out
water plants, tropical ferns and
palms, and just about every

known conifer. For a time
Monserrate boasted the only
lawn in Iberia, and it remains
one of Europe's most richly
stocked gardens, with over a
thousand different species of
subtropical trees and plants.

From the entrance, paths
lead steeply down through
lush undergrowth to a ruined
chapel, half engulfed by a giant
banyan tree. From here, lawns
take you up to Cook's main
legacy, a great **Victorian palace**
inspired by Brighton Pavilion,
with its mix of Moorish and
Italian decoration – the dome
is modelled on the Duomo
in Florence. The interior has
largely been restored after years
of neglect, and you can now
admire the amazingly intricate
plasterwork which covers
almost every wall and ceiling.
The park also has a decent café
(daily 10am–6pm).

### AZENHAS DO MAR

Bus #441 from Sintra (every 1–2hr; 40min). MAP P.117

Whitewashed cottages tumble down the steep cliff face at the pretty village of Azenhas do Mar, one of the most characterful villages of the Sintra coast. The beach is small, but there are artificial seawater pools for swimming in when the ocean is too rough.

### PRAIA DAS MAÇÃS

Bus #441 from Sintra (every 1–2hr; 30min); or Praia das Maças tram from Sintra (see box opposite). MAP P.117

The largest and liveliest resort on this coast, Praia das Maças is also the easiest to reach from Sintra – take the tram for the most enjoyable journey. Along with a big swath of sand, Praia das Maças has an array of bars and restaurants to suit all budgets.

### PRAIA GRANDE

Bus #441 from Sintra (every 1–2hr; 25min). MAP P.117

Set in a wide, sandy cliff-backed bay, this is one of the best and safest beaches on the Sintra coast, though its breakers attract surfers aplenty. In August the World Bodyboarding Championships

are held here, along with games such as volleyball and beach rugby. Plenty of inexpensive cafés and restaurants are spread out along the beachside road, and if the sea gets too rough, there are giant sea pools on the approach to the beach (June–Sept, €10).

### PRAIA DA ADRAGA

No public transport; by car, follow the signs from the village of Almoçageme. MAP P.80 POCKET MAP P.117

Praia da Adraga was flatteringly voted one of Europe's best beaches by a British newspaper; the unspoilt, cliff-backed, sandy bay with just one beach restaurant is certainly far quieter than the other resorts, but it takes the full brunt of the Atlantic, so you'll need to take great care when swimming.

Quaint old trams shuttle from outside Sintra's Museu de Arte Moderna to the coastal resort of Praia das Maças via Colares (April–Sept Fri–Sun four daily, 45min. €2 single). However, check the latest routes and timetables on ☎ 219 233 919 or in the Sintra tourist office, as there are frequent shortenings of the route or alterations to the service.

## CABO DA ROCA

Bus #403 from Sintra or Cascais train stations (every 90min; 45min). MAP P.117

Little more than a windswept rocky cape with a lighthouse, this is the most westerly point in mainland Europe, which guarantees a steady stream of visitors – get there early to avoid the coach parties. You can soak up the views from the café-restaurant and handicraft shop (daily 9.30am–7.30pm) and buy a certificate to prove you've been here at the little tourist office (daily 9am–6.30pm, ☎ 219 280 081).

## CONVENTO DOS CAPUCHOS

☎ 219 237 300; daily: April–Sept 9.30am–8pm; Oct–March 10am–6pm. €5. No public transport. A return taxi from Sintra with a 1hr stopover costs around €30. MAP P.117

If you have your own transport, don't miss a trip to the Convento dos Capuchos, an extraordinary hermitage with tiny, dwarf-like cells cut from the rock and lined with cork – hence its popular name of the Cork Convent. It was occupied for three hundred years until being finally abandoned in 1834 by its seven remaining monks, who must have found the gloomy warren of rooms and corridors too much to maintain. Some rooms – the penitents' cells – can only be entered by crawling through 70cm-high doors; here, and on every other ceiling, doorframe and lintel, are attached panels of cork, taken from the surrounding woods. Elsewhere, you'll come across a washroom, kitchen, refectory, tiny chapels, and even a bread oven set apart from the main complex.

## PENINHA

MAP P.117

With your own transport, it is worth exploring the dramatic wooded landscape between Capuchos and Coba da Roca, much of it studded with giant moss-covered boulders. Some 3km from Capuchos lies Peninha, a spectacularly sited hermitage perched on a granite crag. The sixteenth-century Baroque interior is usually locked, but climb up anyway to get dazzling views of the Sintra coast towards Cascais. You can also take a waymarked 4.5km trail round the crag; otherwise it is a short return walk from the woodland car park.

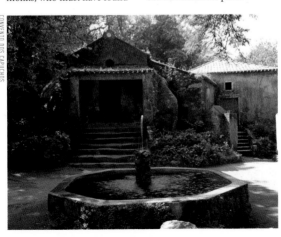

CONVENTO DOS CAPUCHOS

# Restaurants

## ALCOBAÇA

Rua das Padarias 7–11 ☎ 219 231 651. Daily noon–4.30pm & 7pm–midnight. MAP P.113

There's friendly service in the plain, fake-stone dining room, and large servings of grilled chicken, steaks and *bacalhau* dishes from around €10.

## CANTINHO DE SÃO PEDRO

Praça D. Fernando II 18, São Pedro de Sintra ☎ 219 230 267. Daily noon–3pm & 7.30–10pm. MAP P.113

Large restaurant with bare stone walls overlooking an attractive courtyard just off São Pedro's main square. Slightly formal service but excellent food at reasonable prices. On cool evenings a log fire keeps things cosy.

## COLARES VELHO

Largo Dr Carlos de Franca 1–4, Colares ☎ 219 292 727. Tues–Sat 10am–11pm, Sun 10am–8pm.

Delightful restaurant and teahouse in the tiny main square of Colares, on the road between Sintra and the beaches. Traditional Portuguese cuisine, such as *bacalhau*, starts at €15, but it's worth the price; alternatively, take a seat for some fine tea and cakes.

## O LOUREIRO

Esplanada Vasco da Gama, Praia das Maçãs ☎ 219 292 442. Mon–Wed & Fri–Sun 11am–3pm & 7–11pm.

In a prime location overlooking the beach, this is the best place to try good-value local fresh fish and seafood; the grilled squid is always a good and inexpensive choice. The café-bar of the same name opposite is also a good spot for inexpensive drinks.

## PÁTEO DO GARRETT

Rua Maria Eugénia Reis F. Navarro 7 ☎ 219 243 380, ⊛ www.pateodogarrett.com. Mon, Tues & Thurs–Sun 11am–11pm; Jan–April 11am–2pm.

Although this café-restaurant has a dark, dim interior, it's also got a lovely sunny patio offering fine views over the village. Serves standard Portuguese fare from around €12, or just pop in for a drink.

## A TASCA DO MANEL

Largo Dr. Virgílio Horta 5. ☎ 219 230 215. Mon–Sat 10am–10pm. MAP P.113

In total contrast to Sintra's wonderfully ornate Town Hall opposite, this is a very simple little *tasca* with cured hams hanging over the bar. Squeeze into a table for very good-value, no-nonsense fish and grills from under €6.

QUEIJADAS DA SINTRA

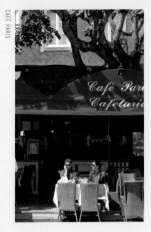

although it is a great place for a cocktail. If you do want to eat, reservations are advised in high season (mains from €15).

## CASA PIRIQUITA

Rua das Padarias 1. Mon, Tues & Thurs–Sun 9am–midnight. MAP P.113
Cosy tearoom and bakery, which can get busy with locals queueing to buy *queijadas da Sintra* (sweet cheesecakes) and other pastries. Further up the hill at no. 18 there's another, more modern, branch, *Piriquita Dois* (closed Tues), which boasts a big outdoor terrace.

## FÁBRICA DAS VERDADEIRAS QUEIJADAS DA SAPA

Volta do Duche 12. Tues–Sun 9am–6pm & 7–9pm. MAP P.113
This old-fashioned café is famed for its traditional *queijadas*, made on the premises for over a century. It's a bit dingy inside, so it's best to buy takeaways to sustain you on your walk to the centre.

# Bars and clubs

## BAR FONTE DA PIPA

Rua Fonte da Pipa 11–13 ☎ 219 234 437. Daily 9pm–2am. MAP P.113
Laid-back bar with low lighting and comfy chairs. It's up the hill from *Casa da Piriquita*, next to the lovely ornate fountain (*fonte*) that the street is named after.

## MAÇAS CLUB

Rua Pedro Álvaro Cabral 2–12, Praia das Maçãs ☎ 219 292 024, ✆ www.macasclub .com. Tues–Sun: 10am–2am, club Fri–Sat 10pm–4am.
Set just off the beach, this café/bar/club is the social hub of the village. There's a fashionable bar area, a karaoke room and separate dancefloor, with guest DJs at weekends.

## TULHAS

Rua Gil Vicente 4 ☎ 219 232 378. Mon, Tues & Thurs–Sun noon–3pm & 7pm–midnight. MAP P.113
Imaginative cooking in a fine building converted from old grain silos – the old grain well takes pride of place in the floor. The giant mixed grills at €24 for two people will keep carnivores more than happy, while the weekend specials are usually excellent with meat and fish from around €9.

# Cafés

## ADEGA DAS CAVES

Rua da Pendoa 2. ☎ 219 239 848. Daily 9am–2am. MAP P.113
Bustling café-bar below *Café Paris* (see below) attracting a predominantly local and youthful clientele; the adjacent restaurant at no. 8 does meals from around €9.

## CAFÉ PARIS

Largo Rainha D. Amélia T219 232 375. Daily 8am–midnight. MAP P.113
This attractive blue-tiled café is the highest-profile in town, which means steep prices for not especially exciting food,

# The Lisbon coast

Lisbon's most accessible beaches lie along the Cascais coast just beyond the point where the Tejo flows into the Atlantic. Famed for its casino, Estoril has the best sands, though neighbouring Cascais has more buzz. The River Tejo separates Lisbon from high-rise Caparica, to the south, on a superb stretch of wave-pounded beach, popular with surfers.

## ESTORIL

With its grandiose villas, luxury hotels and health spa, Estoril (pronounced é-stril) has pretensions towards being a Portuguese Riviera. The centre is focused on the leafy **Parque do Estoril** and its enormous casino (Tues–Sat 3pm–3am; free; semi-formal attire required ; ☎ 214 667 700, ⓦ www.casino-estoril.pt). During World War II, this was where exiled royalty hung out and many spies made their names. Ian Fleming was based here to keep an eye on double agents, and used his experience at the casino as inspiration for the first James Bond novel *Casino Royale*.

The resort's fine sandy beach, **Praia de Tamariz**, is backed by some ornate villas and a seafront promenade that stretches northwest to Cascais,

ESTORIL

a pleasant twenty-minute stroll. In summer, firework displays take place above the beach every Saturday at midnight.

Estoril is also famed for its world-class **golf courses** which lie a short distance inland (info at ⓦwww.portugalgolf.pt); it also hosts the Estoril Open tennis tournament in May (ⓦwww.estorilopen.net).

## Transport to Estoril and Cascais

Trains from Lisbon's Cais do Sodré (every 20min; 35min to Estoril, 40min to Cascais; €1.70 single) wend along the shore. There are also regular buses to and from Sintra, or it's a fine drive down the corniche.

## CASCAIS

MAP BELOW

Cascais (pronounced cash-kaysh) is a highly attractive former fishing village, liveliest round Largo Luis de Camões, at one end of Rua Frederico Arouca, the main mosaic-paved pedestrian thoroughfare. Nearby is the **fish market** (Mon–Fri), best in the afternoon after the catch comes in.

**Praia da Conceição** is the best beach to lounge on or try out watersports. The rock-fringed smaller beaches of **Praia da Rainha** and **Praia da Ribeira** are off the central stretch, while regular buses run 6km northwest to **Praia do Guincho**, a fabulous sweep of surf-beaten sands.

Cascais is at its most charming in the grid of streets north of the **Igreja da Assunção** – its azulejos predate the earthquake of 1755. Nearby, on Rua Júlio Pereiro de Melo, the engaging **Museu do Mar** (☏ 214 815 906; Tues–Sun 10am–5pm; €2.10) relates the town's relationship with the sea, with model boats, treasure from local wrecks, fossils and stuffed fish.

## CASA DAS HISTÓRIAS

Avda Da República 300 ☏ 214 826 970. 🌐 www.casadashistoriaspaularego.com Daily 10am–8pm. Free. MAP BELOW.

The distinctive ochre towers of the modernist **Casa das Histórias** mark a fantastic museum which, unusually, is dedicated to a living artist, Paula Rego. Designed by famous architect Eduardo Souto de Moura, the airy museum features over 120 of her disturbing but beautiful collages, pastels and engravings as well as those by her

FISHING BOAT, CAPARICA

late English husband Victor Willing. Many of her works explore themes of power: women and animals are portrayed as both powerful and sexually vulnerable; men often appear as fish or dressed in women's clothes.

### AROUND CASCAIS MARINA

MAP OPPOSITE

The leafy **Parque Municipal da Gandarinha**, complete with picnic tables and playground, makes a welcome escape from the beach crowds. In one corner stands the mansion of the nineteenth-century Count of Guimarães, preserved complete with its fittings as the **Museu Biblioteca Conde Castro Guimarães** (☎214 825 407, ⓦwww.cm-cascais. pt; Tues–Sun 10am–5pm; closes 1–2pm on Sat and Sun; €2.10, free at weekends). Its most valuable exhibits are rare illuminated sixteenth-century manuscripts.

To the east, the walls of Cascais' largely seventeenth-century fortress (shortly to reopen as a hotel) guard the entrance to the **Marina de Cascais**, an enclave of expensive yachts serviced by restaurants, bars and boutiques.

### CAPARICA

Via Rapida express (hourly; 30min) or slower local buses (every 15–30min; 50min), from Cacilhas or from Lisbon's Areeiro/Praça de Espanha (every 30–60min; 40–60min).

According to legend, Caparica was named after the discovery of a cloak (*capa*) full of golden coins. Today it is a slightly tacky, high-rise seaside resort, but don't let that put you off: it's family friendly, has plenty of good seafood as well as several kilometres of soft sandy beach popular with surfers.

From June to October, buses stop right near the sands – at other times get off at the first stop in Caparica, on the edge of the tree-lined Praça da Liberdade, five minutes from the beach. From here, the pedestrianized Rua dos Pescadores heads down to the seafront.

From the beach, a **narrow-gauge mini-railway** (May–Sept daily every 30min from 9am–7.30pm; €5 return, or €3 return for first nine stops) runs south along the beach for 8km to the smaller resort of **Fonte da Telha**. You can jump off at any of the nineteen stops en route; earlier stops tend to be family-oriented, while later ones are younger, with nudity more or less the norm.

# Restaurants

### O BARBAS

Praia da Costa, Caparica ☎ 212 900 163.
Mon, Tues & Thurs noon–2am.

Not quite the same since it
moved into its two adjacent
modern wood-framed build-
ings, *O Barbas* (*The Beard*) is
nevertheless an atmospheric
beach restaurant with affordable fish, *paella* and *cataplanas*
to die for. You'll probably see
the owner – he's the one with
the huge amounts of facial hair.

### B & B

Rua do Poço Novo 15, Cascais ☎ 214 820
686. Mon–Fri noon–2.30pm & 7–9.45pm, Sat
7–9.45pm. MAP P.124

A small, intimate diner in the
old town, specializing in tender
steaks (around €10). Also does
a few fresh fish dishes and great
desserts – save room for the
chocolate cake.

### JARDIM DOS FRANGOS

Avda Com. Grande Guerra 66, Cascais. Daily
10am–midnight. MAP P.124

Permanently buzzing with

people and sizzling with the
speciality, bargain grilled
chicken from €7, which is
devoured by the plateful at
indoor and outdoor tables. Get
there early to guarantee a table
as it is very popular.

### MUSIC BAR

Largo Praia da Rainha 121, Cascais ☎ 214
820 848. June–Sept daily 10am–10pm; Oct–
May closed Mon. MAP P.124

Great sea views are to be had
inside or out on the raised
terrace at this bustling café-
restaurant. It's a fine spot to
have a sunset beer. It also does
decent, moderately priced fish
and grilled meats (around €12).

### O PESCADOR

Rua das Flores 10, Cascais ☎ 214 832 054.
Daily 12.30–3pm & 7.30–11pm. MAP P.124

The best of a row of lively
restaurants near the fish
market, offering upmarket
seafood – expect to pay over
€20 for superb mains such as
lobster baked in salt or tuna
cooked in olive oil and garlic.

### PRAIA DO TAMARIZ

Praia do Tamariz, Estoril ☎ 214 681 010.
Daily 9am–10pm.

High-profile restaurant right
on the seafront promenade –
which makes the fish, meat and
pasta dishes pretty good value
(mains cost from €15). Also
a great spot for a sangria or
*caipirinha*.

### O SOLAR DO BITOQUE

Rua Regimento 19 de Infantaria Loja
11, Cascais [no phone]. Mon–Sat 10am–
midnight. MAP P.124

*Bitoques* are thin steaks, and
this lively local with outdoor
seating specializes in various
types as well as burgers, salads
and fresh fish. Very good value,
with most dishes under €5.

SURFERS, CAPRICA BEACH

# Cafés

### ESPLANADA SANTA MARTA

Avda Rei Humberto II de Italia, Cascais.
Tues–Sat 10am–10pm. MAP P.124

One of the best places to enjoy
charcoal-grilled fish and savouries, which are served on a tiny
terrace overlooking the sea and
a little beach.

### FAROL DE SANTA MARTA

Rua do Farol, Cascais. Tues–Sun: May–Sept
10am–7pm, Oct–April 10am–6pm. MAP P.124

Attached to a small lighthouse
museum, this little café has
an idyllic suntrap of a terrace,
a perfect spot for a drink
overlooking the sea.

### PASTELARIA BIJOU

Rua Rigimento XIX 55, off Largo Luís de
Camões, Cascais. Daily 9am–9pm. MAP P.124

Simple café in a pretty tiled
building with outside seats on
the square. One of the cheapest
places round here for lunches,
snacks, pastries or drinks.

# Bars and clubs

### CHEQUEURS

Largo Luís de Camões 7, Cascais ☎ 214 830
926. Daily: May–Sept 8am–2am, Oct–April
8am–8pm. MAP P.124

An English-style pub that fills
up early with a good-time

crowd; it serves so-so meals,
too, and shows live soccer on
TV, though most people come
for drinks at tables outside in
the attractive square.

### JONAS BAR

Paredão do Estoril, Monte Estoril. Daily: May–
Sept 8am–2am, Oct–April 8am–8pm. MAP P.124

Right on the seafront just north
of Estoril, this is a laid-back
spot day or night, selling
cocktails, juices and snacks
until the small hours.

### SALAMANDRA BAR

Praia da Duquesa, Cascais ☎ 214 820 287.
Daily noon–2am. MAP P.124

Some 200m from the station
towards Estoril, with a
great view of the seafront,
*Salamandra* has something for
everyone, from bar games to
live TV sports and frequent live
music. Also serves snacks.

### TARQUINHO BAR

Muralha da Praia, Caparica ☎ 212 900 053,
Ⓦ www.tarquinhobar.com. Tues, Wed & Sun
10am–2am, Fri and Sat 9am–2am.

A popular surfers' hangout
right on the seafront promenade, with full meals, snacks,
drinks and cocktails – chill
out on an array of chairs from
deckchairs to bean bags and try
the *caparica especial*, a fine mix
of port and fresh orange.

ACCOMMODATION

# Hotels and guesthouses

Lisbon's hotels range from sumptuous five stars to backstreet hideaways packed with local character. The grander ones tend to be found along Avenida da Liberdade, around Parque Eduardo VII or out of the centre. Better still, opt for one of the places in the Baixa, Alfama or round Bairro Alto from where the centre is a short walk away. Besides hotels, there are pensions (*pensões*; singular *pensão*), guesthouses (*residenciais*; singular *residencial*) and various good-value hostels.

Prices given are for a night in the cheapest double room in high season. Rates drop considerably out of season. Unless otherwise stated, all the places reviewed below have an en-suite bath or shower and include breakfast (anything from bread, jam and coffee to a generous spread of rolls, cereals, croissants, cold meat, cheese and fruit).

## The Baixa and Rossio

**HOTEL AVENIDA PALACE** > Rua 1° de Dezembro 123 Ⓜ Restauradores ☎ 213 218 100, Ⓦ www.hotel-avenida-palace.pt. MAP P.29, POCKET MAP C11 Built at the end of the nineteenth century, and rumoured to have a secret door direct to neighbouring Rossio station, this is one of Lisbon's grandest hotels. Despite extensive modernization, the traditional feel has been maintained with chandeliers and period furniture throughout. There are 82 spacious rooms, each with high ceilings and colossal bathrooms. €200

**HOTEL DUAS NAÇÕES** > Rua da Vitória 41 Ⓜ Rossio ☎ 213 460 710, Ⓦ www.duasnacoes.com. MAP P.29, POCKET MAP D12 Classy, pleasantly faded nineteenth-century hotel with helpful, English-speaking reception staff. Also has rooms for three to four people. €50; €20 extra for en-suite facilities

**HOTEL EVIDENCIA TEJO** > Rua dos Condes de Monsanto 2 Ⓜ Rossio ☎ 218 866 182, Ⓦ www.evidenciatejo.com. MAP P.29, POCKET MAP E11 This historic Baixa townhouse has been given a superb makeover, and now combines bare brickwork with cutting-edge design. Wood-floored rooms aren't huge but come with modems and minibars, and downstairs there is a boutiquey, Gaudi-inspired bar. €130

**HOTEL METRÓPOLE** > Rossio 30, Ⓜ Restauradores ☎ 213 219 030, Ⓦ www.almeidahoteis.com. MAP P.29, POCKET MAP D11 Early twentieth century-era three-star, with an airy lounge bar offering superb views over Rossio and the castle. The simply furnished but spacious rooms are comfortable, but the square can be quite noisy at night. €185

**HOTEL SUÍÇO ATLÂNTICO** > Rua da Glória 9, Ⓜ Restauradores ☎ 213 461 713, Ⓦ www.turimhoteis.com. MAP P.29, POCKET MAP C10 In the last war, this was known to be the spies' favourite hangout – now it's a popular budget hotel in a good location, close to the *elevador* to Bairro Alto. Rooms are fairly standard, though some come with balconies looking down on to seedy Rua da Glória. €68

**PENSÃO GERÊS** > Calçada da Garcia 6 Ⓜ Rossio ☎ 218 810 497, Ⓦ www.

## Booking a room

The main tourist offices (see p.131 for details) can provide accommodation lists, but won't reserve rooms for you. In the summer months, confirm a reservation at least a week in advance and get written confirmation; most owners understand English. Look out, too, for deals on hotel websites which are usually cheaper than walk-in rates.

pensaogeres.com. MAP P.29, POCKET MAP D10. Set on a steep side street just off Rossio, the beautiful, tiled entrance hall and chunky wooden doors set the tone for one of the more characterful central options. The simple rooms of varying sizes are minimally furnished, though all have TV and bathroom. Internet access on request; no breakfast. €55

**PENSÃO PORTUENSE** > Rua das Portas de Santo Antão 149–157 Ⓜ Restauradores ☎ 213 464 197, Ⓦ www.pensaoportuense.com. MAP P.29, POCKET MAP J5. Singles, doubles and triples in a family-run guesthouse in a great position. Recently renovated, all rooms come with a/c and TVs and there's internet access. €65

**RESIDENCIAL FLORESCENTE** > Rua das Portas de Santo Antão 99 Ⓜ Restauradores ☎ 213 426 609, Ⓦ www.residencialflorescente .com. MAP P.29, POCKET MAP J5 The best guesthouse on this pedestrianized street. There's a large selection of air-conditioned rooms across four floors (some en-suite with TV), so if you don't like the look of the room you're shown – and some are very cramped – ask about alternatives. Street-facing rooms can be noisy. There is also a lounge plus internet access for a small fee. €65

**RESIDENCIAL INSULANA** > Rua da Assunção 52 Ⓜ Rossio ☎ 213 427 625, Ⓦ www.insulana.net. MAP P.29, POCKET MAP D12 Go upstairs past a series of shops to reach one of the more appealing Baixa options. With its own bar overlooking a quiet pedestrianized street, the hotel's smart rooms are complete with satellite TV and a/c. English-speaking staff. €65

**VIP EDEN** > Praça dos Restauradores 24 Ⓜ Restauradores ☎ 213 216 600, Ⓦ www.viphotels.com. MAP P.29, POCKET MAP C10 Compact studios and apartments sleeping up to four people are available within the impressively converted Eden cinema. Get a ninth-floor apartment with a balcony and you'll have the best views and be just below the superb breakfast bar and rooftop pool. All come with dishwashers, microwaves and satellite TV. Disabled access. **Studios from €130**

## The Sé, Castelo and Alfama

**ALBERGARIA SENHORA DO MONTE** > Calçada do Monte 39, Tram 28 ☎ 218 866 002, Ⓦ senhoramonte.blogspot. com. MAP P.40–41, POCKET MAP L5 Comfortable, modern hotel in a sublime location with views of the castle and Graça convent from the south-facing rooms, some of which have terraces. Breakfast is taken on the fourth-floor terrace, and private parking is available. Head north from Largo da Graça, taking the first left into Rua Damasceno Monteiro – Calçada do Monte is the first right. €130

**PALACETE CHAFARIZ D'EL REI** > Trav. Chafariz d'El Rei 6, Tram 25 ☎ 218 886 150, Ⓦ www.chafarizdelrei.com. MAP P.40–41, POCKET MAP G12 Luxury guesthouse built in 1909 by a wealthy Brazilian merchant and lovingly restored a century later. From the reception – flooded with light from stained-glass windows – to the mirror room and library, the house is a stunning mix of Brazilian Art Nouveau and neo-Arabic flamboyance. Huge rooms, most with river views, have chandeliers and modern bathrooms while stonking breakfasts keep you going till dinner time. €190

**PENSÃO NINHO DAS ÁGUIAS >**
Costa do Castelo 74 , Tram 12 ☎ 218
854 070. MAP P.40–41, POCKET MAP
E11 Superbly sited in its own view-laden
terrace-garden just below the castle,
this is justifiably one of the most popular
budget places in the city. Climb up
the staircase and past the birdcages.
Rooms are spartan but bright, though
avoid the dingy basement room. Book
in advance as there are only 16 rooms.
No breakfast. €45 for shared facilities,
otherwise €55

**PENSÃO SÃO JOÃO DA PRAÇA >**
Rua de São João da Praça 97–2° & 3°,
Tram 28 ☎ 218 862 591. MAP P.40–41,
POCKET MAP F12 Attractive townhouse
with street-facing wrought-iron balconies.
There's a range of rooms, the best on the
top floor with river views. From €35 with
shared bathroom, up to €55 with bath

**SOLAR DO CASTELO >** Rua das
Cozinhas 2, Bus 37 ☎ 218 870 909,
ⓦ www.heritage.pt. MAP P.40–41,
POCKET MAP F11 A tastefully renovated
eighteenth-century mansion abutting the
castle walls on the site of the former
palace kitchens, parts of which remain.
Its 14 rooms cluster around a tranquil
inner courtyard, where you can enjoy a
vast buffet breakfast. It's not cheap and
rooms aren't enormous, but most boast
balconies overlooking the castle grounds,
and service is second to none. €205

**SOLAR DOS MOUROS** Rua do Milagre
de Santo António 6, Tram 28 ☎ 218 854
940, ⓦ www.solardosmouros.com. MAP
P.40–41, POCKET MAP F12 A tall Alfama
townhouse done out in a contemporary
style with its own bar. Each of the twelve
rooms offers fantastic vistas of the river
(€60 extra) or castle and comes with CD
player and a/c. There's plenty of modern
art to enjoy if you tire of the view. €160;
breakfast €13 extra

# Chiado and
# Cais do Sodré

**HOTEL BAIRRO ALTO >** Praça Luís
de Camões 2 Ⓜ Baixa-Chiado. ☎ 213
408 223, ⓦ www.bairroaltohotel.

com. MAP P.53, POCKET MAP C12 A
grand eighteenth-century building that
has been modernized into a fashionable
boutique hotel. Rooms and communal
areas still have a period feel – the lift
takes a deep breath before rattling up its
six floors – but modern touches appear in
the form of DVDs in rooms, a rooftop café
and a swish split-level bar full of comfy
cushions. €250

**HOTEL BORGES >** Rua Garrett 108
Ⓜ Baixa-Chiado. ☎ 213 461 951,
ⓦ www.lisbonhotelborges.com. MAP
P.53, POCKET MAP C12 In a prime spot
on Chiado's main street, this traditional
and elegantly furnished three-star is very
popular, though front rooms can be noisy.
Double or triple rooms are plain and
small but good value. €90

**HOTEL LISBOA REGENCY CHIADO
>** Rua Nova do Almada 114
Ⓜ Baixa-Chiado. ☎ 213 256 100,
ⓦ www.hotelregencychiado.com.
MAP P.53, POCKET MAP D12 Designed
by architect Álvaro Siza Viera and with
Oriental-inspired interior decor by the
highly rated Portuguese designer Pedro
Espírito Santo, the *Lisboa Regency*
is stylish and uncluttered. Orange
segment-shaped windows give glimpses
of Chiado in one direction and the whole
city in the other. The cheapest rooms
lack much of an outlook, but the best
ones have terraces with stunning views
towards the castle – a view you get from
the bar terrace too. All rooms have wi-fi.
Limited parking available. €200.

# Bairro Alto and
# São Bento

**CASA DE SÃO MAMEDE >** Rua da
Escola Politécnica 159, Bus 1 ☎ 213
963 166, ⓦ www.casadesaomamede
.com. MAP P.62–63, POCKET MAP H5 On
a busy street north of Príncipe Real, this
is a superb eighteenth-century former
magistrate's house with period fittings,
bright breakfast room and a grand
stained-glass window. Rooms are rather
ordinary, but all are equipped with a TV
and a/c. €90

## Author picks

**BUDGET** Lisbon Lounge Hostel p.137
**DESIGNER** Fontana Park p.134
**RETRO CHIC** Heritage Avenida p.134
**FAMILY** Vila Bicuda p.136
**HISTORIC** Palacete Chafariz d'el Rei p.131

**HOTEL ANJO AZUL** > Rua Luz Soriano 75, Bus 1 ☎ 213 478 069, ⓦ www .cb2web.com/anjoazul. MAP P.62–63, POCKET MAP B11 The "Blue Angel" is best known for being gay friendly, but is not exclusively so. Set in a lovely blue-tiled townhouse right in the heart of the area's nightlife, there are 20 simple but attractive rooms set over four floors (€50), some with en-suite facilities (€80). No breakfast; however, there is a communal kitchen. **From €50**

**HOTEL PRINCÍPE REAL** > Rua da Alegria 53, Bus 1 ☎ 213 407 350, ⓦ www.hotelprincipereal.com. MAP P.62–63, POCKET MAP H5 This small four-star sits on a quiet street just below the Bairro Alto. Eighteen rooms, each with modern decor and some with balconies and superb city views. Best of all is the top-floor suite with stunning vistas (€250). **From €130**

**PENSÃO GLOBO** > Rua do Teixeira 37, Bus 1 ☎ 213 462 279, ⓦ www.cb2web .com/pensaoglobo. MAP P.62–63, POCKET MAP B10 Attractive house on a relatively quiet street, bang in the middle of the Bairro Alto. Fifteen varied rooms: all are simple and most are reasonably large with TVs, though avoid those without windows. There's a bar downstairs. No breakfast. **€40**

**PENSÃO LONDRES** > Rua Dom Pedro V 53, Bus 1 ☎ 213 462 203, ⓦ www .pensaolondres.com.pt. MAP P.62–63, POCKET MAP B10 Wonderful old building with high ceilings and 40 pleasant enough rooms sleeping up to four. Some have tiny bathrooms (€70); those without are cheaper (€60), and the best (ask for rooms 402, 409 or 411) have great views over the city. **From €60**

**PENSÃO LUAR** > Rua das Gáveas 101–1°, Bus 1 ☎ 213 460 949 ⓦ www .pensaoluar.com. MAP P.62–63, POCKET MAP C11 Polished interior and decently furnished rooms (with shower and TV) varying in size, so ask to see first. Don't expect a quiet night as the area is packed with bars and restaurants. No breakfast. **€45**

# Estrela, Lapa and Santos

**AS JANELAS VERDES** > Rua das Janelas Verdes 47, Bus 727 or tram 25 ☎ 213 968 143, ⓦ www. heritage.pt. MAP P.75, POCKET MAP G8 Highly recommended, this discreet, eighteenth-century townhouse, where Eça de Queirós was inspired to write Os Maios, is just metres from the Museu de Arte Antiga. Spacious rooms come with marble bathrooms, period furnishings and most with views of the Tejo. Breakfast is served in the delightful walled garden in summer. The top-floor library and terrace command spectacular river views. **€140**

**LAPA PALACE** > Rua do Pau da Bandeira 4 ☎ 213 949 494, ⓦ www. lapapalace.com. MAP P.75, POCKET MAP F7 A stunning nineteenth-century mansion set in its own lush gardens, with dramatic vistas over the Tejo. Rooms are luxurious, and those in the Palace Wing are each decorated in a different style, from Classical to Art Deco. There's also a health club, disabled access and a list of facilities as long as your arm, from babysitting to banqueting. **€275.**

**YORK HOUSE** > Rua das Janelas Verdes 32, Bus 727 or tram 25 ☎ 213 962 435, ⓦ www.yorkhouselisboa.com. MAP P.75, POCKET MAP G7 Located in a sixteenth-century Carmelite convent (and hidden from the main street by high walls), rooms here are chic and minimalist. The best are grouped around a beautiful interior courtyard, where drinks and meals are served in summer, and there's a highly rated restaurant. Advance bookings recommended. **€180**

## Alcântara and Belém

**PESTANA PALACE** > Rua Jau 54, Tram 18 ☎ 213 615 600, Ⓦ www .pestana.com. MAP P.80–81, POCKET MAP C8 Set in an early twentieth-century palace full of priceless works of art, most beds at this five-star hotel are in tasteful modern wings that stretch either side of lush gardens. Most rooms have large terraces and lie a short walk from a sushi bar, a sunken outdoor pool with a fountain to swim out to, and an indoor pool and health club. The price, which can be greatly reduced for summer offers, includes a vast breakfast in the former ballroom. €176

**JERONIMOS 8** > Rua das Jeronimos 8, Tram 15 ☎ 213 600 900, Ⓦ www .jeronimos8.com. MAP P.88–89, POCKET MAP C4 In a great position for Belém's attractions, this hotel is an attractive stone building with boutiquey touches – crisp white decor, marble bathrooms and a modern bar area, plus a substantial buffet breakfast. €200

## Avenida, Parque Eduardo VII and the Gulbenkian

**EUROSTAR DAS LETRAS** > Rua Castilho 6–12 Ⓜ Avenida ☎ 213 573 094, Ⓦ www.eurostarshotels.com. MAP P.96–97, POCKET MAP H5 Modern hotel with its own small gym and bar in a good position between the centre and the Bairro Alto. Rooms come with comfy beds, a choice of pillows and a complicated array of power showers. The best have balconies with downtown views. €140

**FONTANA PARK** > Rua Eng. Viera da Silva 2 Ⓜ Saldanha ☎ 210 410 600, Ⓦ www.fontanapark.com. MAP P.96–97, POCKET MAP J3 This buzzy designer hotel rises sleekly behind the facade of an old steelworks. Chic rooms – the best with terraces – come with Philippe Starck chromatic baths. The communal areas include a restaurant, bar and a courtyard garden with slate walls of running water. Cocktail and sushi nights with guest DJs complete the picture. €215

**HERITAGE LIBERDADE** > Avenida da Liberdade Ⓜ Restauradores ☎ 213 404 040, Ⓦ www.heritage.pt. MAP P.96–97, POCKET MAP J5 In a superb mansion – whose ground floor once sold herbal remedies (the counter still remains) – this hotel superbly blends tradition and contemporary style. Though the dining area/bar is small (and the gym/plunge pool even smaller), the rooms more than compensate with retro fittings and great cityscapes from top-floor rooms. €190

**HOTEL AMAZÓNIA** > Trav. Fábrica dos Pentes 12–20 Ⓜ Rato ☎ 213 877 006, Ⓦ www.amazoniahoteis.com. MAP P.96–97, POCKET MAP G5 This modern, spacious three-star is in a quiet part of town and has a small outdoor pool. Top-floor rooms come with city views, some with balconies. All rooms have satellite TVs and minibars. There's a downstairs bar and restaurant, car parking and disabled access. Breakfast €8. €136

**HOTEL AVENIDA PARK** > Avda Sidónio Pais 6 Ⓜ Parque ☎ 213 532 181, Ⓦ www.avenidapark.com. MAP P.96–97, POCKET MAP H4 Good-sized rooms – beg for one with a view over the park for no extra charge – in a friendly hotel on a quiet street. €80

**HOTEL BRITANIA** > Rua Rodrigues Sampaio 17 Ⓜ Avenida ☎ 213 155 016, Ⓦ www.heritage.pt. MAP P.96–97, POCKET MAP J5 Designed in the 1940s by influential architect Cassiano Branco, this is an Art Deco gem with huge airy rooms, each with traditional cork flooring and marble-clad bathrooms. The hotel interior, with library and bar, has been declared of national architectural importance .A somewhat pricy breakfast is an extra. €135

**HOTEL DOM CARLOS PARQUE** > Avda Duque de Loulé 121 Ⓜ Marquês de Pombal ☎ 213 512 590, Ⓦ www .domcarloshoteis.com. MAP P.96–97, POCKET MAP H4 Decent three-star just off Praça Marquês de Pombal, with fair-sized rooms over eight floors, each with cable TV. Some overlook the neighbouring police and fire stations, which can add to the noise. There's a downstairs bar with plasma TV and garage parking. €116.

**LISBOA PLAZA** > Trav. Salitre 7 Ⓜ Avenida ☎ 213 218 200, Ⓦ www. heritage.pt. MAP P.96–97, POCKET MAP J5 A tasteful, understated former Portuguese family home with marble bathrooms, bar and a fashionable rooftop terrace, a short walk from the main Avenida. Friendly staff and good for families. Limited disabled access. €120

**RESIDENCIAL ALEGRIA** > Praça da Alegria 12 Ⓜ Avenida ☎ 213 220 670, Ⓦ www.alegrianet.com. MAP P.96–97, POCKET MAP J5 Friendly place in a great position, facing the leafy Praça da Alegria ("Happy Square"). Spacious, brightly coloured rooms with TV, though front ones can be noisy. €78

**SANA CLASSIC REX** > Rua Castilho 169 Ⓜ Marquês de Pombal/Parque ☎ 213 882 161, Ⓦ www.sanahotels .com. MAP P.96–97, POCKET MAP G4 One of the less outrageously priced hotels in this neck of the woods – look out for special deals on its website – with small but well-equipped rooms. The best are at the front, sporting large balconies overlooking Parque Eduardo VII. €150

**SHERATON LISBOA** > Rua Latino Coelho 1 Ⓜ Picoas ☎ 213 120 000, Ⓦ www.starwoodhotels.com. MAP P.96–97, POCKET MAP J3 This 1970s high-rise is something of an icon in this part of Lisbon and is now a mecca for those seeking five star spa facilities. The dated exterior hides some very modern attractions including a heated outdoor pool, swanky rooms and a spectacular top -floor bar and restaurant €120

**RESIDENCIAL DOM SANCHO I** > Avda da Liberdade 202–2° Ⓜ Avenida ☎ 213 513 160, Ⓦ www.domsancho .com. MAP P.96–97, POCKET MAP J5 One of the few inexpensive options right on the avenue and, what's more, set in a grand old mansion with high ceilings and decorative cornices – though, as you'd expect, the front rooms are noisy. The large, air-conditioned rooms come with satellite TV. €75

**NH LIBERDADE** > Avda da Liberdade 180B Ⓜ Avenida ☎ 213 514 060, Ⓦ www.nh-hotels.com. MAP P.96–97, POCKET MAP J5 Discreetly tucked into the back of the Tivoli forum shopping centre off the main Avenida, this Spanish chain hotel offers ten floors of modern flair. The best rooms have balconies facing the traditional Lisbon houses at the back. Unusually for central Lisbon, there's a rooftop pool. There's also a bar and restaurant. €155

## Sintra

**CHALET RELOGIO** > Estrada da Pena 22, Sintra-Vila ☎ 219 241 550, Ⓦ www. chaletrelogio.com. MAP P.113 Architect Luigi Mannini, who worked on the Quinta da Regaleira (see p.115), designed this wonderful mansion with a distinctive clock tower. Rooms are simply furnished but enormous, with big windows and high ceilings, and there's a rambling garden too, though it's a long walk to town and you'll need a car. €60

**HOTEL ARRIBAS** > Praia Grande ☎ 219 289 050, Ⓦ www.hotelarribas .pt. MAP P.113 This modern three-star is plonked ungraciously above the beach. Rooms are giant and come with minibars and satellite TV – those with a sea view are hard to fault. There are also seawater swimming pools, a restaurant and café terrace. Also has family rooms sleeping up to four. Disabled access. €120

**PENSÃO NOVA SINTRA** > Largo Afonso d'Albuquerque 25, Estefânia ☎ 219 230 220, Ⓦ www.novasintra. com. MAP P.113 Very smart *pensão* in a big mansion, whose elevated terrace-café overlooks a busy street. The modern rooms all have cable TV and shiny marble floors, and there's a decent restaurant. €80

**PIELA'S** > Avda Desiderio Cambournac 1–3, Estefânia ☎ 219 241 691, Ⓦ www.cafepielas.com. MAP P.113 Popular budget accommodation in a swish, renovated townhouse above a cybercafé, on a busy road. The welcoming English-speaking proprietor offers a range of rooms of varying sizes up to triples. No breakfast. From €60

**RESIDENCIAL SINTRA** > Trav. dos Alvares, São Pedro ☎ & 🖷 219 230 738, Ⓦ www.residencialsintra .blogsopt.com. MAP P.113 The best mid-range option in the area, this rambling old *pensão* has soaring ceilings, wooden floors and oodles of character. There's a substantial garden with a swimming pool and the giant rooms can easily accommodate extra beds – so it's great for families. Book ahead in summer; in winter there's a log fire in the communal lounge. **€80**

**SÃO SATURNIA** > Azóia ☎ 219 283 192, Ⓦ www.saosat.com. MAP P.113 Reached down a steep track – look for the sign left just past the turning to Cabo da Roca, before Azóia – this former convent dates back to the twelfth century and sits in a valley where time seems to stand still. The six rooms, three suites and self-catering apartments are traditionally furnished, while the rambling communal areas are all weathered beams, bare bricks and low ceilings. There's a small outdoor pool, barbecue area, geese, cats, and terraces with stunning views – truly magical. **€170**

## Lisbon coast

**HOTEL BAÍA** > Avda C. Grande Guerra, Cascais ☎ 214 831 033, Ⓦ www .hotelbaia.com. MAP P.124 Large seafront hotel boasting 113 rooms with a/c and satellite TV; front ones have balconies overlooking the beach. There's a great rooftop terrace complete with a covered pool, and a good restaurant. Parking charged extra. **€110/€120 with sea view**

**FAROL DESIGN HOTEL** > Avda Rei Humberto II de Italia 7, Cascais ☎ 214 823 490, Ⓦ www.farol.com .pt. MAP P.124 Right on the seafront, this is one of the area's most fashionable hideaways, neatly combining traditional and contemporary architecture. A new designer wing has been welded onto a sixteenth-century villa, and the decor combines wood and marble with modern steel and glass. The best rooms have sea views and terraces. There's also a restaurant, fairy-lit outside bar and seapool facing a fine rocky foreshore. **€260, or 315 with sea views**

**PERGOLA HOUSE** > Avda Valbom 13, Cascais ☎ 214 840 040, Ⓦ www. pergolahouse.com. MAP P.124 Sumptuous century-old mansion bang in the centre of town with its own garden, stucco ceilings and wonderfully ornate tiled dining room. Each room has its own distinct character, some with their own balconies. **€125**

**PENSÃO REAL** > Rua Mestre Manuel 18, Caparica ☎ 212 918 870, Ⓦ www .hotel-real.pt.. Friendly and reasonable central *pensão*, a few minutes' walk from the beach, just off Rua dos Pescadores. Small but pleasant rooms come with TV and bath and some have balconies and sea views. **€70**

**SOLAR DOM CARLOS** > Rua Latino Coelho 8, Cascais ☎ 214 828 115, Ⓦ www.solardomcarlos.net. MAP P.124 The best-value place in town, set in a sixteenth-century mansion on a quiet backstreet in the pretty western side of Cascais. Dom Carlos once stayed here, hence the royal chapel, which still survives. The tiled interior stays cool in summer, there's a garden and car parking, and the attractive rooms come with satellite TV and fridge. **€70**

**VILA BICUDA** > Rua dos Faisões, Cascais ☎ 214 860 200, Ⓦ www. vilabicuda.com. MAP P.124 A very well run, upmarket villa complex set in its own grounds with two large swimming pools. Excellent for families, the modern villas are well equipped and the complex has its own great café, shop and (pricey) Italian restaurant. But you'll need a car – it's around 3km from central Cascais towards Guincho. **Studios from €125**

# Hostels

Lisbon has some of Europe's best independent hostels, which we list below. A youth hostel card is required for the official Portuguese hostels (*pousadas de juventude*), but you can buy one on your first night's stay. Unless stated, prices do not include breakfast.

**CASCAIS BEACH HOSTEL** > Rua da Vista Alegre 10, Cascais ☎ 309 906 421, ⓦ www.cascaisbeachhostel.com. MAP P.124 In a quiet part of town, ten minutes from the centre, this independent hostel has a small pool and garden as well as a communal lounge, kitchen and internet access. Rooms are a good size with or without bath (€20 extra) – the best have small balconies. No breakfast. **Dorm beds €20, doubles from €50**

**LISBON LOUNGE HOSTEL** > Rua de São Nicolau 13, 4° Ⓜ Rossio ☎ 213 462 061, ⓦ www.lisbonloungehostel .com. MAP P.29, POCKET MAP E12 Understandably popular independent hostel in a great old Baixa townhouse full of stripped floorboards, comfy sofas and books. Free wi-fi and breakfast, occasional film screenings and dinner on request. **Dorm beds €20, twins from €30**

**OASIS HOSTEL** > Rua Santa Catarina 24 Ⓜ Baixa-Chiado/Tram #28 ☎ 213 478 044, ⓦ www.hosteloasis.com. MAP P.53, POCKET MAP A12 In a lovely old townhouse with its own patio garden – complete with palm tree – this welcoming independent hostel is a stone's throw from the fashionable Miradouro Santa Catarina. **Dorm beds €20, doubles from €44**

**POUSADA DE JUVENTUDE DE CATALAZETE** > Estrada Marginal, Oeiras ☎ 214 430 638, ⓦ www. pousadasjuventude.pt. This hostel is set in an eighteenth-century sea-fort overlooking the sea pools in Oeiras, a beach suburb on the train line to Cascais. Reception is open 8am to midnight. Parking available. **Dorms beds €14, twin rooms from €32**

**POUSADA DE JUVENTUDE LISBOA PARQUE DAS NAÇÕES** > Rua de Moscavide 47–101, Parque das Nações, Ⓜ Oriente ☎ 218 920 890, ⓦ www. pousadasjuventude.pt. MAP P.107, POCKET MAP A16. About five minutes' walk northeast of the Torre Vasco da Gama, towards the bridge, this smart, modern youth hostel has a pool table and disabled access. **Dorm beds €17, doubles from €45**

**POUSADA DE JUVENTUDE DE LISBOA** > Rua Andrade Corvo 46 Ⓜ Picoas ☎ 213 532 696, ⓦ www. pousadasjuventude.pt. MAP P.96–97, POCKET MAP H3 The main city hostel, set in a rambling old building, with a small bar (open 6pm to midnight), canteen (reserve meals in advance), TV room and disabled access. There are 30 dorms sleeping four or six people as well as en-suite rooms. Price includes breakfast. **Dorm beds €17, doubles from €45**

**TRAVELLERS HOUSE** > Rua Augusta 89, 1° Ⓜ Baixa-Chiado ☎ 210 115 922, ⓦ www.travellershouse.com. MAP P.29, POCKET MAP D12 Right on Lisbon's main pedestrianized street, this award-winning independent hostel has a wonderful high-ceilinged lounge, bean bags and a DVD room. **Dorm beds €25, doubles from €35**

# Arrival

Lisbon airport is right on the edge of the city and is well served by buses and taxis. The city's train stations are all centrally located and connected to the metro; the main bus station is also close to metro and train stops.

## By air

The aeroporto da Portela (☎ 218 413 700, ⓦ www.aeroportodelisboa.com .pt) is a twenty-minute drive north of the city centre and has a tourist office (daily 7am–midnight, ☎ 218 450 660), a 24hr exchange bureau and left-luggage facilities.

The easiest way in to the centre is by taxi; a journey to Rossio should cost around €15. Prepaid taxi vouchers are also available from the tourist office but, apart from helping you to queue-jump, don't work out any cheaper. Alternatively, catch #91 **Aerobus** (☎ 966 298 558; daily every 20–30min; from 7am–11pm, €3.55, ticket valid for travel on all city buses for that day) from outside the terminal, which runs to Praça dos Restauradores, Rossio, Praça do Comércio and Cais do Sodré train station. **Local bus** #44 also runs to Praça dos Restauradores and Cais do Sodré station (every 10–15min, €1.35), but is less convenient if you have a lot of luggage.

## By train

Long-distance **trains** are run by CP (*Comboios de Portugal*; ☎ 808 208 208, ⓦ www.cp.pt). You'll arrive at Santa Apolónia station, from where you can access the Gaivota metro line or take a bus west to Praça do Comércio. Most trains also call at Oriente station (on the Oriente line) at Parque das Nações This station is more convenient for the airport or northern Lisbon.

## By bus

The national **bus** carrier is Rede Expressos (☎ 707 223 344, ⓦ www .rede-expressos.pt). Most services terminate at Sete Rios, next to the Jardim Zoológico metro stop (for the centre) and Sete Rios train line (for Sintra and the northern suburbs). Many bus services also stop at the Oriente station at Parque das Nações on the Oriente metro line.

## By car

Apart from weekends, when the city is quiet, **driving** round Lisbon is best avoided, though it is useful to hire a car to see the outlying sights. Parking is difficult in central Lisbon. Pay-and-display spots get snapped up quickly and the unemployed get by on tips for guiding drivers into empty spots. It may be easier heading for an official car park, for which you pay around €10 per day. Do not leave valuables inside your car.

# Getting around

Central Lisbon is compact enough to explore on **foot**, but don't be fooled by the apparent closeness of sights as they appear on maps. There are some very steep hills to negotiate, although the city's quirky elevadores (funicular railways) will save you the steepest climbs. Tram, bus and *elevador* stops are indicated by a sign marked "paragem", which carries route details.

Metro stations (ⓜ) are located close to most of the main sights. Suburban trains run from Rossio and Sete Rios stations to Sintra and from Cais do Sodré station to Belém, Estoril and Cascais, while ferries (☎ 218 820 348, ⓦ www.transtejo.pt) link Lisbon's Cais do Sodré to Cacilhas, for the resort of Caparica.

## The metro

Lisbon's efficient **metro** (*Metropolitano*; daily 6.30am–1am; ☎213 558 457, ⊛www.metrolisboa.pt) is the quickest way of reaching the city's main sights, with trains every few minutes. Tickets cost €1.25 per journey, or €0.80 with a Viva Viagem card (see below) – sold at all stations. We've included the official metro map on the inside cover.

## Buses and trams

City trams and buses (daily 6.30am–midnight) are operated by Carris (☎213 613 000, ⊛www.carris.pt). **Buses** (*autocarros*) run just about everywhere in the Lisbon area – the most useful ones are outlined in the box below.

   **Trams** (*eléctricos*) run on five routes, which are marked on the chapter maps. Ascending some of the steepest urban gradients in the world, most are worth taking for the ride alone, especially the cross-city tram #28 (see p.45). Another picturesque route is #12, which circles the castle area via Largo Martim Moniz. Other useful routes are "supertram" #15

## Useful bus routes

**#1** Marquês de Pombal to Belém via Príncipe Real, Cais do Sodré and the docks.

**#2** Night bus from Cais do Sodré to the docks via Santos; until 5am.

**#28** Praça do Comércio to Parque das Nações via Santa Apolónia station.

**#37** Praça da Figueira to Castelo de São Jorge via the Sé and Alfama.

**#44** Outside the airport to Cais do Sodré via Marquês de Pombal, Avda da Liberdade and the Baixa.

**#727** Marquês de Pombal to Belém via Santos and Alcântara.

from Praça da Figueira to Belém (signed Algés), and #18, which runs from Rua da Alfândega via Praça do Comércio to the Palácio da Ajuda. The remaining route, #25, runs from Rua da Alfândega to Campo Ourique via Cais do Sodré, Lapa and Estrela (see p.39).

## Elevadores

There are also four **elevadores**. These consist of two funicular railways offering quick access to the heights of the Bairro Alto (see p.54 & p.60) and to the eastern side of Avenida da Liberdade (p.33); and one giant lift, the Elevador da Santa Justa (see p.32) which goes up to the foot of the Bairro Alto near Chiado.

## Tickets and passes

On board **tickets** cost €1.40 a journey. These are valid on buses, trams, ferries and *elevadores*, though you need to get a separate card for train lines to Sintra or Cascais. Note that the modern tram #15 has an automatic ticket machine on board and does not issue change.

   It's possible just to buy a ticket each time you ride, but **passes**, available from any main metro station, can save you money. First, buy a rechargeable *Viva Viagem* card (€0.50), which you can load up with up to €2–10, after which €0.85 is deducted for each bus or metro journey.

   You can also buy a one-day *1 Dia Rede* pass (€3.70), which allows unlimited travel on buses, trams, the metro and *elevadores* until midnight of the same day.

   If you're planning some intensive sightseeing, the *Cartão Lisboa* (€16 for one day, €27 for two days, or €33.50 for three) is a good buy. The card entitles you to unlimited rides on buses, trams, *elevadores* and the metro as well as entry to or discounts on around 25 museums. It's available from all the main tourist offices.

## Sightseeing tours

**Open-top bus tour** The one-hour "Circuito Tejo" (April–Oct every 30 mins from 9.15am–7.45pm; Nov–March every 45min from 9.45am–5.15pm; €15) takes passengers around Lisbon's principal sights; a day-ticket allows you to get on and off whenever you want. The "Olisipo" tour (April–Oct hourly from 10am–7pm; Nov–March every 45min from 10.15am–5pm; €15) takes in the Parque das Nações (see p.106). Both tours depart from Praça do Comércio. (Information ☎ 213 582 334, ⓦ www.carristur.pt.)

**Tourist tram tour** The "Elétrico das Colinas" (Hills Tour) takes passengers on an eighty-minute ride in an early twentieth-century tram (June–Sept every 30min from 10am–8pm; Oct–May every 40min from 10.20am–5.40pm; €18), departing from Praça do Comércio and touring around Alfama, Chiado and São Bento. (Information on ☎ 213 582 334.)

**River cruises** Two-and-a-half-hour cruises along the Tejo depart from Praça do Comércio's Estação Fluvial (April–Nov daily at 3pm), stopping at Parque das Nações (when tides permit) and Belém. Tickets (€20, includes drink) valid for returns on the later boats. (Information ☎ 218 824 671, ⓦ www.transtejo.pt.)

**Sidecar tours** Get the lowdown on Lisbon in a motorbike sidecar tour; half-day tours from €65 or €95 for two (☎ 963 965 105, ⓦ www.sidecartouring .co.pt).

**Walks** Recommended themed two-hour guided walks are offered by Lisbon Walker (☎ 218 861 840, ⓦ www.lisbonwalker.com; €15), departing daily from Praça do Comércio at 10am, giving expert insight into the quirkier aspects of the city's sites including legends, secret histories and spies.

## Taxis

Lisbon's cream **taxis** have a minimum charge of €2; an average ride across town is €8–13. Fares are twenty percent higher from 10pm to 6am, at weekends and on public holidays. Bags in the boot incur a €1.60 fee. Meters should be switched on, and tips are not expected. Outside the rush hour taxis can be flagged down quite easily, or head for one of the ranks such as those outside the main train stations. At night, it's best to phone a taxi (attracts an extra charge of €0.80): try Rádio Taxis (☎ 218 119 000), Autocoope (☎ 217 996 460) or Teletáxi (☎ 218 111 100).

## Car rental

For more information on driving in Lisbon see p.140. Rental agents include: Alamo/Guerin, ☎ 213 703 400, ⓦ www.alamo.com; Auto Jardim, ☎ 213 549 182, airport ☎ 218 463 187, ⓦ www.auto-jardim.com; Avis, ☎ 213 514 560, airport, ☎ 218 435 550, ⓦ www.avis.com; Budget, ☎ 213 860 516, airport ☎ 218 478 803, ⓦ www.budget.com.pt; Europcar, ☎ 213 535 115, airport ☎ 218 401 176, ⓦ www.europcar.com; Hertz, ☎ 213 812 430, airport ☎ 218 438 669, ⓦ www.hertz.com.

# Directory A–Z

## Addresses

**Addresses** are written in the form "Rua do Crucifixo 50-4°", meaning the fourth storey of no. 50, Rua do Crucifixo. The addition of e, d or r/c at the end means the entrance is on the left (*esquerda*), right (*direita*) or on the ground floor (*rés-do-chão*).

## Cinemas

Mainstream **films** are shown at various multiplexes around the city, usually with Portuguese subtitles. Listings can be found on ⓦ www.agendalx.pt/cinema. The Instituto da Cinemateca Portuguesa, Rua Barata Salgueiro Ⓜ Avenida (☎ 213 596 266 ⓦ www.cinemateca.pt), the national film theatre, has twice-daily shows and contains its own cinema museum.

## Crime

Violent crime is very rare but pickpocketing is common, especially on public transport.

## Electricity

Portugal uses two-pin plugs (230/400v). UK appliances will work with a continental adaptor.

## Embassies and consulates

Australia, Avda da Liberdade 200-2° Ⓜ Avenida; ☎ 213 101 500; Canada, Avda da Liberdade 196-200 Ⓜ Avenida; ☎ 213 164 600; Ireland, Rua da Imprensa à Estrela 1-4°, tram #28 to Estrela; ☎ 213 929 440; South Africa, Avda Luís Bivar 10 Ⓜ Picoas; ☎ 213 192 200; UK, Rua de São Bernardo 33 Ⓜ Rato; ☎ 213 924 000, ⓦ www.uk-embassy.pt; USA, Avda das Forças Armadas, Ⓜ Jardim Zoológico; ☎ 217 273 300.

## Events listings

The best listings magazine is the free monthly *Agenda Cultural* (ⓦ www.agendalx.pt) produced by the town hall (in Portuguese). *Follow me Lisboa* is an English-language version produced by the local tourist office. Both are available from the tourist offices and larger hotels.

## Gay and lesbian travellers

The Centro Comunitário Gay e Lésbico de Lisboa at Rua de São Lázaro 88 (☎ 218 873 918; Wed–Thurs 6–11pm, Fri & Sat 6pm–1am, Ⓜ Martim Moniz) is the main gay and lesbian community centre, run by ILGA whose website (ⓦ www.ilga-portugal.pt) is in English and Portuguese.

## Health

Pharmacies, the first point of call if you are ill, are open Mon–Fri 9am–1pm & 3–7pm, Sat 9am–1pm. Details of **24hr pharmacies** are posted on every pharmacy door, or call ☎ 118. The privately run British Hospital, Rua Saraiva de Carvalho 49 (☎ 213 943 100), has doctors on call 8.30am–9pm. There are various other public hospitals around the city; EU citizens will need form E112.

## Internet

Hotels and **internet cafés** charge around €3–5 per hour for access. Useful central options include: Ponto Net, Lisbon Welcome Centre, Praça do Comércio, Baixa (daily 9am–8pm; ☎ 210 312 810); Web Café, Rua do Diário de Notícias 126, Bairro Alto (daily 4pm–2am; ☎ 213 421 181); and Cyberica, Rua Duques de Bragança 7, Chiado (Mon–Fri 11am–midnight; ☎ 213 421 707).

## Left luggage

There are 24hr lockers at the airport, main train and bus station, charging around €5, depending on size of bag.

## Lost property

Report any loss to the **tourist police** station in the Foz Cultura building in Palácio Foz, Praça dos Restauradores (daily 24hr ☎ 213 421 634). For items left on public transport, contact Carris ☎ 218 535 403.

## Money

Portugal uses the **euro** (€). Banks open Monday to Friday 8.30am–3pm. Most central branches have automatic exchange machines for various currencies. You can withdraw up to €200 per day from ATMs ("Multibanco") – check fees with your home bank.

## Opening hours

Most **shops** open Monday to Saturday 9.30am–7pm; smaller shops close for lunch (around 1–2pm) and on Saturday afternoons; shopping centres are open daily until 10pm or later. Most **museums** and **monuments** open Tuesday to Sunday from around 10am–6pm; details are given in the guide.

## Phones

Most European-subscribed **mobile phones** will work in Lisbon, though you are likely to be charged extra for incoming and outgoing calls. The cheap rate for national and international calls is 9pm–9am Monday to Friday, and all day weekends and public holidays.

## Post

**Post offices** (*correios*) are usually open Monday to Friday 9am–6.30pm. The main Lisbon office at Praça dos Restauradores 58 is open until 8pm (☎ 213 238 700). Stamps (*selos*) are sold at post offices and anywhere that has the sign "Correio de Portugal – Selos" displayed.

## Smoking

In common with most other EU countries, smoking is prohibited in most restaurants and cafés.

## Sports

Lisbon boasts two of Europe's top **football** teams, Benfica (ⓦ www.slbenfica.pt) and Sporting (ⓦ www.sporting.pt). Fixtures and news on ⓦ www.portuguesesoccer.com. The area also contains some of Europe's best **golf courses**, especially around Cascais and Estoril (info at ⓦ www.portugalgolf.pt). The Atlantic beaches at Caparica and Guincho are ideal for **surfing** and windsurfing, and international competitions are frequently held there (details on ⓦ www.surfingportugal.com). **Horse-riding** is superb in the Sintra hills, and skilled horsemanship can also be seen at Portuguese **bullfights** (see Praça de Touros, p.101). The Estoril Open in April draws **tennis** fans to the city (ⓦ www.estorilopen.net), and thousands of runners hit the streets for the **Lisbon Marathon** (ⓦ www.maratonclubeportugal.cm), held in September.

## Telephone information

A free telephone information line gives basic tourist information in English (Mon–Sat 9am–midnight, Sun 9am–8pm, ☎ 800 781 212).

## Tickets

You can **buy tickets** for Lisbon's theatres and many concerts from the ticket desk in FNAC in the Armazéns do Chiado shopping centre (see p.56), Valentim de Carvalho on Rua do Carmo 28, as well as from the main venues themselves. Online tickets can be purchased from ⓦ www.ticketline.pt or blueticket.pt.

## Time

Portuguese **time** is the same as Greenwich Mean Time (GMT). Clocks go forward an hour in late March and back to GMT in late October.

## Tipping

Service charges are included in hotel and restaurant bills. A ten-percent tip is usual for restaurant bills, and hotel porters and toilet attendants expect at least €0.50.

## Toilets

There are very few **public toilets** in the streets, although they can be found in nearly all main tourist sights (signed variously as *casa de banho*, *retrete*, *banheiro*, *lavabos* or "WC"), or sneak into a café or restaurant if need be. Gents are usually marked "H" (*homens*) or "C" (*cabalheiros*), and ladies "M" (*mulheres*) or "S" (*senhoras*).

## Tourist information

Lisbon's main **tourist office** is the Lisbon Welcome Centre at Praça do Comércio (see map on p.28; daily 9am–8pm; ☏ 210 312 810, ⓦ www.visitlisboa.com), which can supply accommodation lists, bus timetables and maps.

Tourist offices at the airport (see p.140) and at Santa Apolónia station (Tues–Sat 7.30am–1pm, ☏ 218 821 606) can help you find accommodation, as can a few smaller "Ask Me" kiosks dotted around town, like the ones on Rua Augusta and opposite Belém's Mosteiro dos Jerónimos (both daily 10am–1pm & 2–6pm). There is also the Y Lisboa tourist office at Rua Jardim do Regedor 50 (daily 10am–8pm, ☏ 213 472 134), with information geared up to young and student travellers.

There are also tourist offices in all the main **day-trip destinations**: Sintra Turismo (see map, p.113; daily: June–Sept 9am–8pm, Oct–May 9am–7pm; ☏ 219 231 157, ⓦ www.cm-sintra.pt); Estoril Turismo (opposite the train station; daily: June–Sept 9am–8pm, Oct–May 9am–7pm; ☏ 214 663 813, ⓦ www.visitestoril.com); Cascais Turismo (see map, p.124; Mon–Sat 9am–7pm, Sun 10am–6pm; ☏ 214 868 204); and Caparica Turismo (Avda da República 18; closed Mon–Fri 1–2pm, Sat afternoon and Sun; ☏ 212 900 071).

## Travel agents

The well-informed Top Atlantico, Rua do Ouro 109 (☏ 213 403 220, ⓦ www.topatlantico.pt), Baixa, also acts as an American Express agent.

## Travellers with disabilities

Lisbon airport offers a service for **wheelchair-users** if advance notice is given (☏ 213 632 044), while the Orange Badge symbol is recognized for disabled car parking. The main public transport company, Carris, offers an inexpensive dial-a-ride minibus service, *O Serviço Especial de Transporte de Deficientes* (€1.40 per trip; Mon–Fri 6.30am–10pm, Sat & Sun 8am–10pm; ☏ 213 613 141, ⓦ www.carris.pt), though two days' advance notice and a medical certificate are required.

## Water

Lisbon's **water** is technically safe to drink, though you may prefer bottled water. Inexpensive bottled water is sold in any supermarket, though tourist shops and restaurants charge considerably more.

# Festivals and events

## CARNIVAL

**February–March**
Brazilian-style parades and costumes, mainly at Parque das Nações.

## PEIXE EM LISBOA

**March–April** W www.peixemlisboa.com
Lisbon's annual fish festival takes place at the Pavilhão de Portugal, Parque das Nações and includes masterclasses by top chefs.

## ROCK IN RIO LISBOA

**May (even yearly)** W www.rockinrio-lisboa.sapo.pt
Five-day mega rock festival in Parque Bela Vista, in the north of the city.

## SANTO ANTONIO

**June**
Lisbon's main festival is for its adopted saint, Santo António. On June 12 there's a parade down Avenida da Liberdade followed by a giant street party in the Alfama.

## GAY PRIDE

**June** W www.arraialpride.ilga-portugal.pt
Lisbon's increasingly popular gay pride event (Arraial Pride) changes venues but has recently been held at Praça do Comércio.

## SINTRA MUSIC FESTIVAL

**June–July** W www.estorilportugal.com/events
Performances by international orchestras and dance groups in and around Sintra, Estoril and Cascais.

## SUPERBOCK SUPERROCK

**July** W www.superbock.pt
One of the country's largest rock festivals, with local and international bands in various venues, sometimes on the Lisbon coast.

## JAZZ NUMA NOITE DE VERÃO

**August** W www.musica.gulbenkian.pt
Big annual (Jazz on a Summer Night) festival at the Gulbenkian's open-air amphitheatre.

## FESTIVAL DOS OCEANOS

**August** W www.festivaldosoceanos.com
A series of concerts and ocean-themed environmental events takes place at various riverside venues throughout August.

## SÃO MARTINHO

**November 11**
St Martin's Day is celebrated with the first tasting of the year's wine accompanied with hot chestnuts.

## CHRISTMAS (NATAL)

The main Christmas celebration is midnight Mass on December 24, which is followed by a meal of *bacalhau*.

## NEW YEAR'S EVE (ANO NOVO)

The best place for New Year's Eve is Praça do Comércio, where fireworks light up the riverfront.

## Public Holidays

In addition to Christmas (Dec 24–25) and New Year's Day (Jan 1) public holidays include Shrove Tuesday (Feb/March); Good Friday (March/April); April 25 (Liberty Day); May 1 (Labour Day); June 10 (Portugal/Camões Day); June 12 (Santo António); August 15 (Feast of the Assumption); October 5 (Republic Day); November 1 (All Saints' Day); December 1 (Independence Day); December 8 (Immaculate Conception).

# Chronology

**60 BC** > Julius Caesar establishes Olisipo as the capital of the Roman Empire's western colony.

**711** > Moors from North Africa conquer Iberia, building a fortress by the *alhama* (hot springs), now known as Alfama.

**1147** > Afonso Henriques, the first king of the newly established Portuguese state, retakes Lisbon from the Moors and builds a cathedral on the site of the former mosque.

**1495–1521** > The reign of Dom Manuel I coincides with the golden age of Portuguese exploration. So-called "Manueline" architecture celebrates the opening of sea routes. The 1494 Treaty of Tordesillas gives Spain and Portugal trading rights to much of the globe.

**1498** > Vasco da Gama returns to Belém with spices from India, which helps fund the building of the monastery of Jeronimos.

**1581** > Victorious after the battle of Alcántara, Philip II of Spain becomes Filipe I of Portugal, and Portugal loses its independence.

**1640** > Portuguese conspirators storm the palace in Lisbon and install the Duke of Bragança as João IV, ending Spanish rule.

**1706–50** > Under João V, gold and diamonds from Brazil kick-start a second golden age; lavish building programmes include the Aqueduto das Águas Livres.

**1755** > The Great Earthquake flattens much of Lisbon. The Baixa is rebuilt in "Pombaline" style, named after the Marquês de Pombal.

**1800s** > Maria II (1843–53) rules with German consort, Fernando II, and establishes the palaces at Ajuda and Pena in Sintra. Fado becomes popular in the Alfama. Avenida da Liberdade is laid out.

**1900–10** > Carlos I is assassinated in Lisbon in 1908, while two years later, the exile of Manuel II marks the end of the monarchy and birth of the Republic.

**1932–68** > Salazar's dictatorship sees development stagnate. Despite massive rural poverty, elaborate "New State" architecture includes the Ponte 25 de Abril, originally named Ponte de Salazar.

**1974** > April 25 marks a largely peaceful Revolution. Former Portuguese colonies are granted independence, leading to large-scale immigration.

**1986** > Entry to the European Community enables a rapid redevelopment of Lisbon.

**1990s** > Lisbon's role as Capital of Culture (1994) and host of Expo 98 helps fund a metro extension, the Ponte Vasco da Gama and the Parque das Nações.

**2000–05** > In 2004 Lisbon hosts the European Football Championships in two new soccer stadia. Fado star Mariza brings the music to an international audience.

**2005–2010** > EU leaders sign the Lisbon Treaty on Dec 13, 2007, agreeing a draft constitution. A new high-speed rail line is approved between Lisbon and Madrid.

# Portuguese

English is widely spoken in most of Lisbon's hotels and tourist restaurants, but you will find a few words of Portuguese extremely useful. Written Portuguese is similar to Spanish, though pronunciation is very different. Vowels are often nasal or ignored altogether. The consonants are, at least, consistent:

## CONSONANTS

**c** is soft before e and i, hard otherwise unless it has a cedilla – *açucar* (sugar) is pronounced "assookar".

**ch** is somewhat softer than in English; *chá* (tea) sounds like Shah.

**j** is like the "s" in pleasure, as is g except when it comes before a "hard" vowel (a, o and u).

**lh** sounds like "lyuh".

**q** is always pronounced as a "k".

**s** before a consonant or at the end of a word becomes "sh", otherwise it's as in English – Cascais is pronounced "Kashkaish".

**x** is also pronounced "sh" – Baixa is pronounced "Baisha".

## VOWELS

**e/é**: e at the end of a word is silent unless it has an accent, so that *carne* (meat) is pronounced "karn", while *café* is "caf-ay".

**ã or õ**: the tilde renders the pronunciation much like the French -an and -on endings, only more nasal.

**ão**: this sounds something like a strangled "Ow!" cut off in midstream (as in *pão*, bread – *são*, saint – *limão*, lemon).

**ei**: this sounds like "ay" (as in *feito* – finished)

**ou**: this sounds like "oh" (as in *roupa* – clothes)

# Words and phrases

## BASICS

| | |
|---|---|
| sim | yes |
| não | no |
| olá | hello |
| bom dia | good morning |
| boa tarde/noite | good afternoon/night |
| adeus | goodbye |
| até logo | see you later |
| hoje | today |
| amanhã | tomorrow |
| por favor/se faz favor | please |
| tudo bem? | everything all right? |
| está bem | it's all right/OK |
| obrigado/a | thank you (male/female speaker) |
| onde | where |
| que | what |
| quando | when |
| porquê | why |
| como | how |
| quanto | how much |
| não sei | I don't know |
| sabe...? | do you know...? |
| pode...? | could you...? |
| há...? (silent "h") | is there...? there is |
| tem...? pron. "taying") | do you have...? |
| queria... | I'd like... |
| desculpe | sorry |
| com licença | excuse me |
| fala Inglês? | do you speak English? |
| não compreendo | I don't understand |
| este/a | this |
| esse/a | that |
| agora | now |
| mais tarde | later |
| mais | more |
| menos | less |
| grande | big |
| pequeno | little |
| aberto | open |
| fechado | closed |
| senhoras | women |
| homens | men |
| lavabo/quarto de banho | toilet/bathroom |

## GETTING AROUND

| | |
|---|---|
| esquerda | left |
| direita | right |
| sempre em frente | straight ahead |
| aqui | here |
| ali | there |
| perto | near |
| longe | far |
| Onde é... | Where is ... |
| a estação de camionetas? | the bus station? |
| a paragem de autocarro para... | the bus stop for... |
| Donde parte o autocarro para...? | Where does the bus to...leave from? |
| A que horas parte? (chega a...?) | What time does it leave? (arrive at...?) |
| Pare aqui por favor | Stop here please |
| bilhete (para) | ticket (to) |
| ida e volta | round trip |

## COMMON SIGNS

| | |
|---|---|
| aberto | open |
| fechado | closed |
| entrada | entrance |
| saida | exit |
| puxe | pull |
| empurre | push |
| elevador | lift |
| pré-pagamento | pay in advance |
| perigo/perigoso | danger/ous |
| proibido estacionar | no parking |
| obras | (road) works |

## ACCOMMODATION

| | |
|---|---|
| Queria um quarto | I'd like a room |
| É para uma noite (semana) | It's for one night (week) |
| É para uma pessoa (duas pessoas) | It's for one person/ two people |
| Quanto custa? | How much is it? |
| Posso ver? | May I see/ look? |
| Há um quarto mais barato? | Is there a cheaper room? |
| com duche | with a shower |

## SHOPPING

| | |
|---|---|
| Quanto é? | How much is it? |
| banco; câmbio | bank; change |
| correios | post office |
| (dois) selos | (two) stamps |
| Como se diz isto em Português? | What's this called in Portuguese? |
| O que é isso? | What's that? |
| saldo | sale |
| esgotado | sold out |

## DAYS OF THE WEEK

| | |
|---|---|
| Domingo | Sunday |
| Segunda-feira | Monday |
| Terça-feira | Tuesday |
| Quarta-feira | Wednesday |
| Quinta-feira | Thursday |
| Sexta-feira | Friday |
| Sábado | Saturday |

## MONTHS

| | |
|---|---|
| Janeiro | January |
| Fevereiro | February |
| Março | March |
| Abril | April |
| Maio | May |
| Junho | June |
| Julho | July |
| Agosto | August |
| Aetembro | September |
| Outubro | October |
| Novembro | November |
| Dezembro | December |

## USEFUL WORDS

| | |
|---|---|
| azulejo | glazed, painted tile |
| cais | quay |
| capela | chapel |
| casa | house |
| centro commercial | shopping centre |
| estação | station |
| estrada/rua | street/road |
| feira | fair or market |
| igreja | church |
| jardim | garden |
| miradouro | viewpoint/belvedere |
| praça/largo | square |

## NUMBERS

| | |
|---|---|
| um/uma | 1 |
| dois/duas | 2 |
| três | 3 |
| quatro | 4 |
| cinco | 5 |
| seis | 6 |
| sete | 7 |
| oito | 8 |
| nove | 9 |
| dez | 10 |
| onze | 11 |
| doze | 12 |
| treze | 13 |
| catorze | 14 |
| quinze | 15 |
| dezasseis | 16 |
| dezassete | 17 |
| dezoito | 18 |
| dezanove | 19 |
| vinte | 20 |
| vinte e um | 21 |
| trinta | 30 |
| quarenta | 40 |
| cinquenta | 50 |
| sessenta | 60 |
| setenta | 70 |
| oitenta | 80 |
| noventa | 90 |
| cem | 100 |
| cento e um | 101 |
| duzentos | 200 |
| quinhentos | 500 |
| mil | 1000 |

# Food and drink terms

## BASICS

| | |
|---|---|
| assado | roasted |
| colher | spoon |
| conta | bill |
| copo | glass |
| cozido | boiled |
| ementa | menu |
| estrelado/frito | fried |
| faca | knife |
| garfo | fork |
| garrafa | bottle |
| grelhado | grilled |
| mexido | scrambled |

## MENU TERMS

| | |
|---|---|
| pequeno almoço | breakfast |
| almoço | lunch |
| jantar | dinner |
| ementa turística | set menu |
| prato do dia | dish of the day |
| especialidades | speciality |
| lista de vinhos | wine list |
| entradas | starters |
| petiscos | snacks |
| sobremesa | dessert |

## SOUPS, SALAD AND STAPLES

| | |
|---|---|
| açucár | sugar |
| arroz | rice |
| azeitonas | olives |
| batatas fritas | chips/french fries |
| caldo verde | cabbage soup |
| fruta | fruit |
| legumes | vegetables |
| massa | pasta |
| manteiga | butter |
| molho (de tomate/ piri-piri) | tomato/chilli sauce |
| omeleta | omelette |
| ovos | eggs |
| pão | bread |
| pimenta | pepper |
| piri-piri | chilli sauce |
| queijo | cheese |
| sal | salt |
| salada | salad |
| sopa de legumes | vegetable soup |
| sopa de marisco | shellfish soup |
| sopa de peixe | fish soup |

## FISH AND SHELLFISH

| | |
|---|---|
| atum | tuna |
| camarões | shrimp |
| carapau | mackerel |
| cherne | stone bass |
| dourada | bream |
| espada | scabbard fish |
| espadarte | swordfish |
| gambas | prawns |

| | |
|---|---|
| lagosta | lobster |
| lulas (grelhadas) | squid (grilled) |
| mexilhões | mussels |
| pescada | hake |
| polvo | octopus |
| robalo | sea bass |
| salmão | salmon |
| salmonete | red mullet |
| santola | spider crab |
| sapateira | crab |
| sardinhas | sardines |
| tamboril | monkfish |
| truta | trout |
| viera | scallop |

## MEAT

| | |
|---|---|
| alheira | chicken sausage |
| borrego | lamb |
| chanfana | lamb or goat casserole |
| chouriço | spicy sausage |
| coelho | rabbit |
| cordeiro | lamb |
| dobrada/tripa | tripe |
| espetada mista | mixed meat kebab |
| febras | pork steaks |
| fiambre | ham |
| fígado | liver |
| frango no churrasco | barbecued chicken |
| leitão | roast suckling pig |
| pato | duck |
| perdiz | partridge |
| perú | turkey |
| picanha | strips of beef in garlic sauce |
| presunto | smoked ham |
| rim | kidney |
| rodizio | barbecued meats |
| rojões | cubed pork cooked in blood with potatoes |
| vitela | veal |

## PORTUGUESE SPECIALITIES

| | |
|---|---|
| açorda | bread-based stew (often seafood) |
| arroz de marisco | seafood rice |
| bife à portuguesa | thin beef steak with a fried egg on top |
| caldeirada | fish stew |
| bacalhau à brás | salted cod with egg and potatoes |
| bacalhau na brasa | dried cod roasted with potatoes |
| bacalhau a Gomes Sá | dried cod baked with potatoes, egg and olives |
| cataplana | fish, shellfish or meat stewed in a circular metal dish |
| cozido à portuguesa | boiled casserole of meat and beans, served with rice and vegetables |
| feijoada | bean stew with meat and vegetables |
| migas | meat or fish in a bready garlic sauce |
| porco à alentejana | pork cooked with clams |

## SNACKS AND DESSERTS

| | |
|---|---|
| arroz doce | rice pudding |
| bifana | steak sandwich |
| bolo | cake |
| gelado | ice cream |
| pastel de nata | custard tart |
| pastéis de bacalhau | dried cod cakes |
| prego | steak sandwich |
| pudim | crème caramel |

## DRINKS

| | |
|---|---|
| um copo/uma garrafa de/da... | a glass/bottle of... |
| vinho branco/tinto | white/red wine |
| cerveja | beer |
| água (sem/com gás) | mineral water (without/with gas) |
| fresca/natural | chilled/room temperature |
| sumo de laranja/maçã | orange/apple juice |
| chá | tea |
| café | coffee |
| sem/com leite | without/with milk |
| sem/com açúcar | without/with sugar |

## PUBLISHING INFORMATION

This first edition published April 2011 by **Rough Guides Ltd**

80 Strand, London WC2R 0RL

11, Community Centre, Panchsheel Park, New Delhi 110017, India

**Distributed by the Penguin Group**

Penguin Books Ltd, 80 Strand, London WC2R 0RL

Penguin Group (USA) 375 Hudson Street, NY 10014, USA

Penguin Group (Australia) 250 Camberwell Road, Camberwell, Victoria 3124, Australia

Penguin Group (NZ) 67 Apollo Drive, Mairangi Bay, Auckland 1310, New Zealand

Rough Guides is represented in Canada by Tourmaline Editions Inc. 662 King Street West, Suite 304, Toronto, Ontario M5V 1M7

Typeset in Minion and Din to an original design by Henry Iles and Dan May.

Printed and bound in China

© Matthew Hancock 2011

Maps © Rough Guides

160pp includes index

A catalogue record for this book is available from the British Library

ISBN 978-1-84836-256-7

1 3 5 7 9 8 6 4 2

## ROUGH GUIDES CREDITS

**Text editor:** Andy Turner

**Layout:** Dan May

**Cartography:** Katie Lloyd-Jones

**Picture editor:** Mark Thomas

**Photographers:** Matthew Hancock, Natascha Sturny

**Production:** Rebecca Short

**Proofreader:** Jan McCann

**Cover design:** Chloë Roberts, Dan May

## THE AUTHOR

**Matthew Hancock** fell in love with Portugal when he was a teacher in Lisbon. He later returned to the country to walk the 775-mile Portuguese-Spanish border. Now a journalist and editor living in Dorset, he is also the author of the Rough Guides to the Algarve and Madeira and co-author of the *Rough Guide to Portugal* and the *Rough Guide to Dorset, Hampshire and the Isle of Wight*.

# HELP US UPDATE

We've gone to a lot of effort to ensure that the first edition of **Pocket Rough Guide Lisbon** is accurate and up-to-date. However, things change – places get "discovered", opening hours are notoriously fickle, restaurants and rooms raise prices or lower standards. If you feel we've got it wrong or left something out, we'd like to know, and if you can remember the address, the price, the hours, the phone number, so much the better.

Please send your comments with the subject line "**Pocket Rough Guide Lisbon Update**" to ❷ mail@roughguides.com. We'll credit all contributions and send a copy of the next edition (or any other Rough Guide if you prefer) for the very best emails.

Have your questions answered and tell others about your trip at ❿ www.roughguides.com

# PHOTO CREDITS

All photography by Matthew Hancock & Natascha Sturny © Rough Guides except the following:
Front cover: Monument to the Discoveries © Tom Mackie Pictures Colour Library
Back cover: Rua Garrett/Largo do Chaido © Renaud Visage/Corbis
Title page: View over the Alfama district © Banana Pancake/Alamy
Full page: Tram #28 © Bloomberg/Getty Images
p.2 Rua Augusta © Michele Falzone/Corbis
p.3 Terraco Bar © Michele Falzone/Corbis
p.6 Igreja de Santa Engracia © Yadid Levy/Corbis
p.8 Pasteis de Nata © Michele Falzone/Corbis
p.8 Tram #28 © Mark Thomas
p.9 Torre de Belém © PCI/Alamy
p.9 Bairro Alto nightlife © Andy Christiani/Alamy
p.11 Oceanário © Hans Georg Roth/Corbis
p.11 Palácio da Pena © Marco Simoni/Getty Images
p.13–14 Tiled map © Mark Thomas
p.15 Mosteiro dos Jerónimos © Gustavo Figueiredo/ Turismo de Lisboa
p.15 Castelo de São Jorge © Gustavo Figueiredo/ Turismo de Lisboa
p.17 The Temptations of St Anthony by Hieronymous Bosch © MNAA

p.17 Casa das Histórias © Luis Ferreira Alves
p.19 Grilled prawns © Sean Russell/Getty Images
p.20 Lux nightclub © Luisa Ferreira/Lux Club
p.21 Portas Largas © LOOK/Alamy
p.24 Mercado da Ribeira © Yadid Levy/Alamy
p.25 Manuel Tavares © Cro Morgan/Alamy
p.26–27 Mosteiro dos Jerónimos © Marco Simoni/Corbis
p.31 View over the Baxia District © Luis Veiga/ Getty Images
p.32 Elevador de Santa Justa © Mark Thomas
p.33 Elevador do Lavra © Mark Thomas
p.64 Bairro Alto nightlife © Forget Gautier/ Alamy
p.73 Traditional fado guitar © Turismo de Lisboa/ Gustavo Figueiredo
p.74 Basílica Estrela © Sylvain Grandadam/ Corbis
p.76 Museu Nacional de Arte Antigua © MMNA
p.81 Museu do Oriente interior © Meseu do Oriente
p.90 Torre de Belém © Mark Thomas
p.101 Praça de Touros © Martin Jones/Corbis
p.103 Eleven restaurant © Eleven Restaurant
p.116 Palácio da Pena © Marco Simoni/Corbis
p.123 Estoril coast © Turismo de Lisboa
p.138–139 Rossio Station © Mark Thomas

# Index

Maps are marked in **bold**.

SO NOW WE'VE TOLD YOU
ABOUT THE THINGS NOT TO
MISS, THE BEST PLACES TO
STAY, THE TOP RESTAURANTS,
THE LIVELIEST BARS AND THE
MOST SPECTACULAR SIGHTS,
IT ONLY SEEMS FAIR TO
TELL YOU ABOUT THE BEST
TRAVEL INSURANCE AROUND